KNOW YOUR BIBLE QUIZ BOOK

by

Amos R. Wells

BAKER BOOK HOUSE
Grand Rapids, Michigan

Previously published in 1927 by W. A. Wilde Company
under the title, *Know Your Bible?*

ISBN: 0-8010-9523-9

PHOTOLITHOPRINTED BY CUSHING - MALLOY, INC.
ANN ARBOR, MICHIGAN, UNITED STATES OF AMERICA
1973

INTRODUCTION

Everybody who uses this book is going to be per—fect—ly dee—lighted with it. But not at first. Oh, no; not at first.

At first, most of the people who use this book are going to be disgusted with themselves or with the author or both. They are going to find out how much—or how little—they know about the Bible. They are likely to discover that it is "how little" rather than "how much."

And they are going to blame it on me. They are going to say, "What fool questions! I could answer any sensible set of questions about the Bible, but these—pah!" Ours is an age of alibis.

All I can say is that if any one can get up a set of fifteen hundred questions on the Bible, covering all parts of it, and include a larger number of easy questions than I have included, I'd like to see him do it. I'd just like to see him do it.

I've tried to ask fifteen hundred questions which any one ought to be able to answer if he really knows his Bible; if he is acquainted—not with the minutiæ of the Bible, but with its broad general outlines. These questions do not call for a knowledge of genealogical tables, but of the chief Bible characters. They do not call for the details of Jewish history, and not a single date is asked for in all the fifteen hundred queries; but they do insist upon a knowledge of the Bible's most significant and interesting events, from cover to cover. The questions are not theological—perhaps some would find them easier if they were, for then they could air their theories; but they call for an acquaintance with the most beautiful and uplifting sentences and passages in all the sixty-six books of the Bible, the inspired wisdom on which all theology is based—or ought to be.

Said one on whom I tried these questions, and who failed lamentably, "What's the use of such questions, anyway?" No use, unless there is use in knowing the Bible, being at home in all parts of it, forming an acquaintance with Bible persons and happenings, becoming able to recognize Bible references in literature, and gradually absorbing the lofty Bible ideals. Many people, to judge from such tests as these questions afford, find "no use" in the Bible beyond the twenty-third Psalm, the Lord's Prayer, the Beatitudes, the Ten Commandments (hazily remembered), and, in cases of extreme proficiency, the fourteenth chapter of John.

The more you use this book the more you will see the use of it. Using it, especially if you read the Bible references zealously, will gradually familiarize you with the Bible, with the whole Bible. You will begin to feel actually at home in the Book of books. Its splendor will grow upon you. You will be amazed by its variety, as you discover all kinds of literary forms in the Sacred Library, and you will begin to realize that it is indeed the literature of one of the most brilliant of races. You will be constantly hitting upon fascinating stories which you did not know were in the Bible. Before long you will be filled with wonder at the wisdom of the Book. You will see in it the summary of rules for success and happiness, peace and prosperity, a perfect guide for social well being, a statesman's manual, a comprehensive treatise on human life. And at last you will perceive with awe that this is not like other volumes; that through it God is speaking to you; that its words reach into the eternities and up to the infinite; that its pages acquaint you with the Father, and with his matchless love revealed through his only begotten Son. And so I dare to hope for an evangelistic outcome of these questions.

But don't be afraid of them.

"Who was Maher-shalal-hashbaz?"

Few of these questions are as hard as that.

"Where was Christ born?"

Not all of them are as easy as that.

Most of them lie between the two extremes, and somewhere between the two extremes most readers will find themselves and their friends.

No matter. You want to know the Bible, and this is a good way to go about it. You must begin from your present state of knowledge or of ignorance. The essential thing is to begin. Then, having begun, the essential thing is to keep on.

Start with the First Series and grade yourself two points for every question you answer with a fair degree of accuracy. Be easy with yourself at first—you'll need it. After a while, you may increase your rigor.

Then go on to the Second Series, and so on till you have graded yourself on all thirty of them. Fifteen hundred questions at two per cent each means 3,000 per cent for a perfect score. You'll be lucky if you get 1,000.

The problem is to lift that 1,000—or 500, or whatever—up to 3,000. Tackle the problem, for it is well worth tackling.

Begin again with Series One and see how much you can remember. Your first grade may have been 30 on that Series, and now it is 50, perhaps even 60 or 70; splendid progress! You feel the glow of achievement. Bible knowledge is within your grasp. You gallop on through all of the thirty Series. Your score is now 2,000, an improvement of 100 per cent. Glorious!

You can hardly refrain from trying the questions on your family, on your friends and acquaintances. But wait just a little. Be canny. The full exhilaration of superiority comes only when you can reel off all the questions—or practically all—and know all the answers without having to look in the back of the book. Then you can exult in your new-found knowledge and make no mention of its newness. Then you can inquire after Maher-shalal-hashbaz with an assurance that will impress every one within sound of your learned voice. Review the book till you have attained 3,000 per cent, or have come within sight of it.

Then launch yourself on an unarmed world.

Tackle Sunday-school teachers. Expose their shallow pretensions without pity. Do not leave them till they cry for mercy, and ask where they can get a copy of this book.

Tackle infidels, or those who pretend to be infidels, and show them how little they know about the book they have been condemning.

Tackle the real Bible lovers. They will surprise and delight you with their proficiency, and in their turn they will be glad to be introduced through these questions to parts of the Bible which perhaps they have been neglecting.

Use the book on your Sunday-school class. They will find these questions as interesting as the jolliest game they ever played.

Inveigle some member of your family into the affair, some friend or a mere acquaintance. Ask the questions of each other. Get up a vigorous contest. See which one can get a hundred first in any Series; then in five Series, in ten, in the entire thirty.

Try it on your young people's society. Set a number of the members to studying the book for an old-fashioned "spell-down," only the questions will take the place of the words given out to spell. There is material here for a capital social entertainment.

It goes without saying that you have in these fifteen hundred innocent queries a fine answer to the problem of Sunday afternoons and of the home evenings.

The entire Bible has been laid under contribution for these questions—every Book, almost every chapter and page. No one can be ready with these fifteen hundred answers and not gain a first-rate knowledge of his Bible.

The text used is the King James—not because it is the most accurate translation, for it is not, but because it is the Bible which has entered into the literature and life of the race, and for all purposes except exact study it will never be displaced.

The author of this book has left a few mistakes in it,—say three, or may be two,—because nothing tickles the readers of a book of this sort more than to discover an error in it, and we aim to please.

The Quizzes in the back of the book present a grouping of the questions under twenty-one different classifications. They are for the use of teachers and others who wish to stimulate Bible study along specific lines; Bible geography, for instance. After the book is mastered in the usual way, it will prove freshly interesting to take the Quizzes and tackle it from their new viewpoints.

It is hoped, also, that the use of these questions will stimulate many to read the Bible straight through from the first word of Genesis to the last word of Revelation. Many wonderful discoveries will be made in the course of the journey, and Bible knowledge will be knit together into a unified and vitalized whole. After this is done, the next thing might well be the reading of some Bible history, such as that by Blaikie, or Edersheim, or Stanley, or Geikie.

In short, the aim of this little book is to furnish recreation in the first place, but in the second place to arouse in the reader so great an enthusiasm for the Book of Books that he will not rest content with the answers to questions, even the answers to so many as fifteen hundred questions, but will go jubilantly on in the pursuit of the Bible knowledge which means the knowledge of the Son of God, the blessed Redeemer of the World.

AMOS R. WELLS.

Auburndale, Mass.

SERIES I

1. What famous town is five miles south of Jerusalem?_________
2. Who said, "Thou art the man"?_____________________________
3. What Book of the Bible tells about the rebuilding of the wall of Jerusalem?____
4. In connection with what two great events is hyssop mentioned?
____
5. Finish the quotation: "Ho, every one that thirsteth."_________
____
6. Which of the brothers of Jesus wrote Books of the New Testament? ____
7. Give exactly "the Golden Rule."_____________________________
____
8. What European city first heard Christian preaching?_________
9. Name the three famous Johns of the New Testament.__________
____
10. Of what rich man did Satan ask the question, "Doth he fear God for nought?"____
11. What general sacrificed his daughter in fulfilment of his vow?
____
12. The story of what prophet is connected with a gourd?_________
13. What is the best-known Bible reference to a pearl?___________
____
14. Who was Jacob's favorite wife?_____________________________
15. What was the duty of the Levites?__________________________
16. What is the highest mountain in Palestine?__________________

17. Complete the proverb, "A wise son maketh________________."
18. Who was pulled out of a dungeon by cords eased with rotten rags? ____
19. Where is the tree whose leaves are "for the healing of the nations"? ____
20. Who wrote about "the valley of the shadow of death"?______
____
21. In what Book of the Bible is the benediction beginning, "Now unto him that is able to keep you from falling"? ____________
22. Where in the Bible is the famous description of the power of the tongue?____
23. Where in the Bible is a vivid picture of a thunderstorm?______
____
24. Repeat Christ's saying about idle words.__________________
____
25. Where was the burning bush?_____________________________
26. Who was Peter's brother?_________________________________
27. Who in Europe was the first to become a Christian?__________
28. What Psalm did Moses write, and how does it begin?_________
____
29. Who was Mordecai?____
30. On what occasion did two bears kill forty-two children?______
____
31. What was the brazen serpent?______________________________
____
____
32. What is the "love chapter" of the Bible?___________________
33. What is the longest chapter of the Bible?___________________
34. What is the whole sentence, "pleased not himself?"__________
____

35. What is the longest river in Palestine?____________________

36. How many thousands did Christ feed at one time? And on another occasion how many thousands? ____________________

37. What was Matthew's other name?____________________

38. Who was David's great friend?____________________

39. What is the Decalogue?____________________

40. Complete the verse: "O come, let us worship and bow down."
____

41. What is the rest of the verse beginning, "Now faith is the substance of things hoped for"?____________________

42. Who led the way to the place of the Last Supper?____________
____

43. What was the food of John the Baptist in the wilderness?____
____

44. What are the other names of the Sea of Galilee?____________
____

45. "Bear ye one another's burdens"—what is the rest?__________
____

46. Who saw the famous vision of the deepening waters?________

47. To what does the Psalmist compare a large family of children?
____

48. What king was hidden in the temple for the first six years of his life?____________________

49. Who was the mother of Moses?____________________

50. What is the first tree definitely named in the Bible?__________
____

SERIES II

1. Who was Elkanah? ____________________
2. Distinguish between Amoz and Amos. ____________________
____
3. Finish the quotation: "The Lord knoweth the way of the righteous: but ____________________."
4. Who were the three most famous of the human ancestors of Christ? ____________________
5. What is the Hexateuch? ____________________
6. Which is the most famous of the metrical paraphrases of the Psalms? ____________________
7. Who said, "I am not ashamed of the gospel of Christ"? ______
8. Who was the principal Hanani of the Bible? ____________________
9. What Book of the Bible means "the Going Forth"? __________
10. What King "loved husbandry"? ____________________
11. What letters did Paul write to churches in Macedonia? ________
____
12. What were created on the six days of creation? ____________
____
13. Who was the husband of Mary the mother of Jesus? __________
14. Who offered "strange fire" before the Lord? ____________
15. What four Books were originally called the Books of the Kings? ____________________
16. How was John the Baptist clothed? ____________________
____

17. What king of Israel injured himself fatally by falling through the lattice of an upper chamber?------------------------------

18. Name the twelve tribes of Israel.------------------------------

----

----

19. In what land was the Book of Deuteronomy spoken and written? --

20. Which of the disciples lived the longest?--------------------

21. What were the leaders of Israel called after the death of Joshua? --

22. What does the name, "Jesus," mean?------------------------

23. What is the exact title of the last Book of the Bible?----------

----

24. Who succeeded Moses as leader of Israel?------------------

25. Finish the quotation: "For the law was given by Moses, but --."

26. Who was the first man, and what does his name mean?------

----

27. To whom did the Lord say, "Be strong and of good courage"?

----

28. What heathen tribe once captured the ark of the covenant?---

----

29. What great general of the Old Testament had a name which means the same as "Jesus"?------------------------------

30. Who was the heathen god of flies?--------------------------

31. What two Gospels were written by Paul's assistants?---------

----

32. To what great leader did the Lord say, "Ye have dwelt long enough in this mount," and what was the mount?------------

33. Who was the wicked daughter of the wicked Jezebel?---------

34. What country had a king of whom it is said that he "knew not Joseph"? ______________

35. Of whom was it said, "In him was life; and the life was the light of men"? ______________

36. Which tribe was divided, half on one side of the Jordan and half on the other? ______________

37. Who bored a hole in the lid of a chest to receive gifts for the repair of the temple? ______________

38. Where was Jesus born? ______________

39. To the Christians of what famous Grecian commercial city did Paul write two letters? ______________

40. Finish Paul's prayer, "That the word of the Lord may have free course, and ______________."

41. What famous Bible reference to a shoe lace? ______________
____

42. Where did Isaiah live? ______________

43. What Books parallel the two Books of Kings? ______________

44. What Jewish queen had a name which means the planet Venus? And what was her original Jewish name? ______________

45. Who wrote, "My God, my God, why hast thou forsaken me?" and on what occasion was it quoted? ______________
____

46. Where was Galatia? ______________

47. What tribe led the first attack on the Canaanites, and why?
____

48. What king received from the Lord the sign of the shadow going backward on a dial? ______________

49. What tribe escorted the tabernacle on the marches through the wilderness? ______________

50. Of what New Testament Book is the author unknown? ______________

SERIES III

1. What New Testament Book was written first?----------------
2. What Jewish leader was cupbearer to a king?----------------
3. Who gave the exhortation to "pray without ceasing"?--------
4. What other Book was written by the author of the third Gospel, and for whom did he write both Books?-----------------
5. What is the Pentateuch?------------------------------------
6. What famous woman was among the human ancestors of Christ? --
7. What King of Judah profaned the temple and was punished with leprosy?--
8. Finish the sentence: "The fool hath said in his heart--------."
   ----
9. What Book of the Bible tells about the origin of the Sabbath?
   ----
10. Distinguish between Zacharias and Zechariah.
11. How many years did the Israelites spend in the wilderness?
12. What Hebrew king killed himself after a defeat in battle? And what was the battle?--------------------------------
13. Of whom is it said that he "walked with God: and he was not; for God took him"?-------------------------------------
14. Where was the church whose members were divided, some being followers of Paul, some of Apollos, some of Cephas, and some of Christ?-------------------------------------
15. Who is called "the weeping prophet"?-----------------------

16. What in secular history is the name of Ahasuerus, the husband of Esther?____
17. What is the meaning of *El* in Hebrew names, as Daniel, Elisha, Elisabeth? ____
18. In what connection are taskmasters most prominently mentioned in the Bible?______________________________________
19. Who wrote a prophecy based upon a vivid description of a plague of locusts?______________________________________
20. For whom did John write the Revelation?____________________
21. Where was Bashan?____
22. When did Paul spend three years in Arabia?_________________
23. Among the children of a Hebrew family, who was especially consecrated, and why?______________________________________
24. Who said "Let patience have her perfect work"?_____________
25. Who was the great Hebrew statesman of the Exile?___________
26. Where is it said, "They part my garments among them, and cast lots upon my vesture," and with what great event is the saying connected?______________________________________
27. What river does the Bible call "the great river"?____
28. What is said by the Psalmist to be "the beginning of wisdom"? ____
29. Who was Zephaniah?______________________________________
30. Who said, "Drink waters out of thine own cistern"?__________
31. How was Elijah taken up into heaven?____
32. What Bible verse strongly urges meditation on Bible truth? ____
33. Repeat the comforting verse based on the distance between the east and the west.______________________________________

34. Who was the father of Noah?______________________________

35. Complete the quotation: "The ox knoweth his owner, and the ass his master's crib: but______________________________."

36. Who said that Christ would baptize with the Holy Ghost?____

37. Why were Adoni-bezek's thumbs and great toes cut off by the Israelites? ______________________________

38. Who was Abishag?______________________________

____

39. Who is called "the brightness of his (God's) glory, and the express image of his person," and in what Book is the expression? ______________________________

40. To what tribe did Moses belong?______________________________

41. What was Dagon?______________________________

____

42. Who was Elisabeth?______________________________

43. Who was king of Judæa when Christ was born?______________

44. Distinguish between Hannah and Anna.____________________

____

____

45. What Hebrew prophet had fire fall from heaven and consume two bands of fifty each, sent out against him?_______________

46. Who was Adonijah?______________________________

47. Who was Achsah?______________________________

48. Who said, "It is not for you to know the times or the seasons," and on what occasion?______________________________

49. Who wrote, "The just shall live by faith," and in what Book is it found?______________________________

50. What did Saul's armorbearer do when he saw that his master was dead?______________________________

SERIES IV

1. What city had a name meaning "Thessalian victory"?--------
2. Give the names of Nehemiah's chief enemies.----------------
3. What Bible man lived the longest, and how long did he live?
----
4. Finish the sentence: "The lines are fallen unto me-----------
---."
5. What Book of the Bible means "Beginning"?----------------
6. Where in the Bible are the fierce "bulls of Bashan" mentioned?
7. Who was Peninnah?------------------------------------
8. What five books of the Bible have only one chapter each?----
----
9. Where was Eden?--------------------------------------
10. What is the proverb about a man diligent in his business?----
----
----
11. Who was "the voice of one crying in the wilderness"?---------
----
12. What king, in using symbolic arrows, showed his lack of energy? ---
13. Where is the great prophecy of Christ the Suffering Servant?
----
14. Who insisted on accompanying Elijah on his last journey?----
----
15. Where in the Bible is the vision of the wheels within wheels?
----

16. What babe was hidden in a basket of rushes?________________
17. Who was called the Lamb of God, and who called him that?

____

18. What mount is a Sabbath day's journey from Jerusalem?______

____

19. At what age did the Levites begin their service in the temple and what age did they end it?______________________________

____

20. Complete Paul's sentence: "Wherein thou judgest another,___"

____

21. Whose head was fastened in the temple of Dagon?___________
22. What Bible Book is named for the Levites?_________________
23. What was "that great and terrible wilderness"?_____________

____

24. What were the Hebrew names of Daniel's three friends?______
25. Where was Kadesh-Barnea?________________________________
26. What did Christ, hanging on the cross, do for his mother?____

____

27. What New Testament city was named after the prophet Nahum? ____
28. What and where was Shushan (Susa)?_____________________

____

29. To whom was the promise made, "The Lord thy God is with thee whithersoever thou goest"?____________________________
30. Who was Timothy?____
31. What Bible Book has for its sub-title, "The Preacher"?________
32. What is the world's most famous poem?_____________________
33. Who spoke of "the foolishness of preaching"?________________
34. What was "the city of palm trees"?__________________________

35. Who wrote, "Rend your heart, and not your garments, and turn unto the Lord your God"?______________________________
36. What is the New Testament form of Jonah?________________
37. Where is the famous account of the industry of the ant?_______
____
38. Who are said to be "ministering spirits"?___________________
39. What was the ancient name of Bethel?______________________
40. Who were the magi?____
____
41. Finish the quotation, "Cease to do evil______." Who wrote it?
____
42. What Greek convert did Paul once take with him to Jerusalem? ____
43. What Book describes the siege and fall of Jerusalem?_________
____
44. What was it that two cows without drivers brought back to the Israelites? ____
45. What form did the Holy Spirit take at Christ's baptism?_______
____
46. Who was the mother of Solomon?_____________________________
47. What New Testament character was a Nazirite?_______________
48. Who was the great prophet of David's time?_________________
49. Who is spoken of as "the faithful witness"?_________________
50. For what is Anathoth most noted?___________________________

SERIES V

1. Complete the quotation: "The heavens declare__________; and the firmament showeth__________________________________."
2. Name the seven churches of Asia________________________________

   ____
3. What great Jewish prophets were captives in Babylonia? _____

   ____
4. What event had to do with Adam's rib?____________________

   ____
5. What is the meaning of *iah* in the termination of Hebrew names, as Zephaniah, Hezekiah?______________________________
6. How many Epistles of John in the New Testament?__________
7. Who said, "Ye shall be witnesses unto me," and to whom did he say it?____
8. What tribe took the place before God of all the Hebrew first-born? ____
9. Who were Hophni and Phinehas?__________________________
10. Who was the father of Methuselah?_______________________
11. What is the shortest Book of the Bible?____________________
12. What was Pithom?_______________________________________
13. What was a burnt offering?_________________________________
14. What is probably the oldest city in Palestine?________________
15. What is the chief mention of a star in the Bible?____________

    ____
16. How did the Israelites isolate lepers?_______________________

    ____

17. How many times in Christ's life did a voice from heaven testify to him?
18. Who was Vashti?
19. Of what New Testament character was it foretold that he should have "the spirit and power of Elijah"?
20. What two Israelites alone of their generation were allowed to enter Canaan, and why?
21. The names of what two archangels are in the Bible?
22. What was "the upper room"?
23. Complete the quotation: "The earth is the Lord's, and the fulness thereof."
24. For what deed is Rahab remembered?
25. Who were the first to bring disciples to Jesus?
26. Quote a Bible verse condemning snobbishness, "respect of persons."
27. What does "Selah" mean in the Psalms?
28. What very fat king oppressed the Israelites?
29. Fill out this quotation: "The foolishness of God is . . . . and the weakness of God is . . . ."
30. Where is Hebron?
31. Who was Cephas?
32. Locate the expression, "Vanity of vanities."
33. Why were the men of Beth-shemesh smitten?
34. "Unstable in all his ways"—what is the whole of that sentence?

35. What characterized the laws of the Medes and Persians?______
____

36. Why is Christ called Alpha and Omega?__________________
____

37. What were "the horns of the altar," and what was their significance? ______________________________________

38. Who said, "I am crucified with Christ"? ________________

39. Where in the Bible is the most vivid picture of a sluggard?__
____

40. Complete the sentence: "This is a faithful saying, and worthy of all acceptation that________________________________."

41. How many disciples were in Jerusalem immediately after Christ's ascension? ______________________________

42. Who was Othniel?______________________________

43. What disciple was chosen to take the place of Judas and complete the Twelve?______________________________

44. Supply the missing words: "Though your sins be as scarlet, they shall be . . . . . .; though they be red like crimson, they shall be . . . . . ."______________________________

45. What prophet is repeatedly called "son of man" in his own Book? ______________________________________

46. Finish the sentence, "How shall we escape, if we neglect ______
____."

47. Who were the "sons of the prophets"?____________________

48. What food did Daniel and his friends obtain to take the place of the king's wine, meat, and dainties?__________________

49. "Let us not be weary in well doing"—what is the rest of Paul's sentence? ______________________________________

50. Who compared the Israelites to "broken cisterns that can hold no water"? ______________________________________

SERIES VI

1. Who are the two boys whose coats are especially mentioned in the Bible?________________

2. What was the "Asia" of the New Testament?________________

____

3. Who are the major prophets?________________

4. In what Book is the saying, "The people had a mind to work"?

____

5. From what city did the Israelites send spies into Canaan?____

____

6. Why is the Book of Numbers so called?________________

7. Where in the Bible is the command that a man shall "leave his father and his mother, and shall cleave unto his wife"?____

____

8. What good king of Judah worked with Isaiah?________________

9. Where in the Bible is the fullest account of heaven?__________

____

10. Finish the verse: "Let the words of my mouth, and the meditation of my heart________________"

11. What is the other name of the Mount of Olives?________________

12. What is the shortest verse of the Bible and where is it found?

____

13. Of what time is it said, "There were giants in the earth in those days"? ________________

14. What three gifts did the wise men offer to the infant Jesus?

____

15. Who were Bael and Ashtoreth?________________

16. What two notable periods of forty days each in the life of Christ? ____________________

17. What was the name of Moses' sister?____________________

18. What is the Fourth Commandment, in brief?____________________
____

19. What three Bible characters were let down through windows over city walls?____________________

20. Of what disciples are we told their occupations?____________________
____

21. What town did Christ make his headquarters during his public ministry?____________________

22. Name Noah's three sons.____________________

23. Who foretold the time when men should beat their swords into ploughshares and their spears into pruning hooks?____________________
____

24. Name the two sons of Zebedee.____________________

25. Repeat the Aaronic benediction.____________________

26. What was the meal offering?____________________

27. How do we know that Simon Peter was married?____________________
____

28. What is the verse of the Psalms which speaks of the death of God's saints?____________________

29. Who said to Christ, "If thou wilt, thou canst make me clean"?
____

30. How does Egypt come into the story of Christ?____________________
____

31. Give the dimensions of Noah's ark.____________________

32. What is "the beginning of wisdom," according to the proverb?
____

33. Who called herself "the handmaid of the Lord"?____________________

34. What is Jeremiah's famous saying about the people who insist that everything is peaceful when the opposite is the case?_____
____
35. Who was Og?____
36. In what Book is the sentence, "There is no new thing under the sun"? ____
37. What is "the Benedictus"?______________________________
38. Who was killed in spite of the fact that he clung to the horns of the altar?____
39. What is the first half of the quotation which ends: "and exalted them of low degree"?______________________________
40. What prophet foretold the time when "your sons and your daughters shall prophesy, your old men shall dream dreams, your young men shall see visions"?___________________________
41. Of what miracle was Elijah's mantle the instrument?________
____
42. Who is called "the dayspring from on high," and by whom?
____
43. Who asked, "Can any good thing come out of Nazareth?" ____
44. What prophet was bidden to eat the roll of a book?__________
45. Who captured Jerusalem and made it his capital?___________
46. What is "the Magnificat"?______________________________
47. What king dreamed a dream and required his wise men to tell not only what it meant but what it was?_______________
48. What did Zechariah foretell when he prophesied of the fountain that should be opened "to the house of David and to the inhabitants of Jerusalem for sin and for uncleanness"? ______
49. Where did Jonah seek to go when running away from his duty, and from what port did he set sail?_________________________
50. Who was Haman?_______________________________________

SERIES VII

1. What Book means "the Second Law"?
2. Name the twelve minor prophets.
3. Where may we find the benediction beginning, "The Lord hear thee in the day of trouble"?
4. What was the length of a "Sabbath day's journey"?
5. Who was the first woman?
6. What three great men lived in Hebron?
7. What book of the Bible has the largest number of chapters?
8. With whom do you associate the sentence, "Speak, Lord; for thy servant heareth"?
9. What king issued a solemn decree that every man should bear rule in his own house?
10. What was the biggest thing that Andrew ever did?
11. Who said, "I am doing a great work, so that I cannot come down"?
12. What living creatures did Noah take into the ark?
13. What disciple was called by Christ "an Israelite indeed, in whom is no guile"?
14. Who compared the Jewish law to a schoolmaster?
15. Why was Pentecost (meaning "Fiftieth") so named?

16. What is the beginning of the quotation, "but godliness is profitable unto all things"?______________________________________
17. What was Christ's first miracle, and where was it performed?
____
18. What is the Sixth Commandment?____________________________
19. Of whom is it said that they had all things in common?_______
____
20. What is wrong with these references: Ahaziah 6:23; 3 John 2:1; 3 Peter 4:8?____
21. How many times did Christ drive the traders out of the temple? ____
22. Complete the sentence beginning, "The word of God is quick and powerful, and____."
23. How many verses in the shortest Psalm?______________________
24. Where was John when he wrote the Revelation?______________
____
25. What was "the gift of tongues"?_____________________________
26. How long a rain made Noah's flood?___________________________
27. Of whom is it said that a sharp two-edged sword went out of his mouth?____
28. What were the Urim and Thummim?__________________________
29. Whither did Moses flee after he had killed the Egyptian?______
____
30. What deliverer of the Israelites was left-handed?_____________
31. Of what church is it said that daily additions were made to its membership? ____
32. What did Solomon choose when the Lord, in a dream, offered him whatever he might desire?________________________________
33. Who were furthered in their wooing by aiding maidens in drawing water at wells?_______________________________________

34. What did the Israelites erect to commemorate the passing of the Jordan?____
35. Of what church was Paul speaking when he said that he determined to know nothing among them but "Jesus Christ, and him crucified"?____
36. When two women laid claim to a child, how did Solomon decide between them?____
37. Which of the Judges won his victory using only an ox goad for a weapon?____
38. What did the passover commemorate?____________________
39. Who succeeded Elijah?__________________________________
40. Finish the Beatitude: "Blessed are the meek_________________."
41. What present was once made to David so precious that he at once offered it to the Lord?__________________________________
42. Of whom was the stirring question asked, "Who knoweth whether thou art come to the kingdom for such a time as this?" ____
43. Finish the quotation: "Eye hath not seen, nor ear heard, neither have entered into the heart of man__________________."
44. Finish the quotation: "When thou saidst, Seek ye my face,____ ____."
45. For what is "the house of Abinadab in the hill" famous?______ ____
46. Where did Noah's ark rest?______________________________
47. Complete the proverb: "A false balance is____________: but a just weight is__________." ________________________________
48. For what is Mt. Pisgah noted?_____________________________
49. Finish the saying: "Wisdom excelleth folly, as far as________."
50. Who was hailed as "the chariot of Israel and the horsemen thereof"? ____

SERIES VIII

1. What woman was paid for nursing her own baby?__________

____

2. What great event occurred at Pentecost?__________

____

3. Finish the proverb, "The fear of the Lord is__________."
4. What two prominent mentions of ravens in the Bible?__________

____

5. With what Bible story is a scarlet thread associated?__________

____

6. Where was "the flaming sword which turned every way"?__________

____

7. For what is Mizpah (Mizpeh) in Benjamin noted?__________

____

8. What was the peace offering?__________

____

9. What is the significance of the Bible phrase, "Every man under his vine and under his fig tree"?__________
10. For what is Shiloh noted?__________
11. What prophet rendered a spring healthful by putting salt into it? __________
12. Who said, "Should such a man as I flee"?__________
13. What, in brief, is the Tenth Commandment?__________
14. Who was the father-in-law of Moses?__________
15. Who, when about to dare a perilous deed, said, "If I perish, I perish"? __________

16. Quote a proverb which gives a rule for safety.________________
____
17. What does the Book of Lamentations describe as "new every morning"? ____
18. What common symbol of peace is connected with the Flood?
____
19. Who said, to those who seek the Lord, "Thou shalt find him, if thou seek him with all thy heart and with all thy soul"?______
20. What is the beginning of the sentence which ends "__________ in the light of the Lord"?____________________________________
21. In what battle did the Israelites win a victory through the thundering of the Lord?____________________________________
22. Finish the sentence: "When my father and my mother forsake me ____."
23. Who was Zipporah?____
24. Whom does the Bible call the wisest man?_________________
25. When and where did the fall of manna cease?________________
26. In what Book is the sentence, "To everything there is a season"? ____
27. What was Daniel's Chaldean name?_________________________
28. What general was encouraged by the vision of a man with a drawn sword in his hand?___________________________________
29. What is meant when people say of a man that he is "a regular Jonah"? ____
30. Complete the Beatitude: "Blessed are the pure in heart______."
31. Name the two sons of Moses.______________________________
32. Finish the verse: "The Lord is good, a strong hold in the day of trouble; and he_________."______________________________
33. What promise did God make when the Flood was over?______
____

34. Finish the quotation, "The harvest is past, the summer is ended, and____."
35. Who was Sisera?____
36. What prophet was bidden to lie on his left side 390 days and on his right side 40 days, each day for a year of his nation's iniquity? ____
37. Who was Aaron?____
38. What prophet saw the vision of a stone cut out of the mountain without hands?____
39. Explain the line of the hymn, "Here I raise my Eben-ezer."____
____
40. How was the palsied man, borne by four friends, brought before Jesus?____
41. What did the Israelites mean by "unclean" beasts and birds?__
____
42. Of whom was it said, "He knew what was in man"?__________
43. What was "the massacre of the innocents"?__________________
____
44. At what gate of the temple was the lame man lying who was healed by Peter and John?_________________________________
45. When does the passover begin? How long does it last?_______
46. Who was Emperor of Rome when Christ was born?__________
47. What determined how long the Israelites in their wanderings should camp in one place?_________________________________
____
48. Where was Christ's home for the first thirty years of his life?
____
49. Finish Joel's eloquent phrase: "Multitudes, multitudes_______."
50. "This is the day which the Lord hath made"—finish the verse.
____

SERIES IX

1. What is the significance of the phrase, "From Dan to Beer-sheba"? --
2. What heathen general had nine hundred iron war chariots?--
3. How many proverbs did Solomon speak?------------------
4. What is the rest of the proverb, "Surely in vain the net is spread --"?
5. What prophet foretold the massacre of the Bethlehem children? --
6. Who was the first boy?------------------------------------
7. Who succeeded Herod the Great as ruler of Judæa?----------
8. What was the origin of the saying, "Hitherto hath the Lord helped us"?--
9. Of whom was it said that he and his assistants "read in the book in the law of God distinctly, and gave the sense, and caused them to understand the reading"?------------------
10. Complete the sentence: "Let God be true, but----------------."
11. What two Books contain the Ten Commandments?----------
12. What city wall fell at a blast from rams' horns and a great shout? --
13. What prophetess lived under a palm tree?------------------
14. What does the proverb say about "the liberal soul"?----------
----
15. Finish the quotation: "I have planted,------------watered, but God --."

16. With what sentence about a cord does Ecclesiastes recommend friendship? ________________

17. What medicine was found in Gilead?________________

18. Who was the first king of Israel, and whose son was he?________________

19. Where in the Bible is the most complete list of fashionable female apparel?________________

20. Who was greatly blessed by keeping the ark in his house three months? ________________

21. What did Paul say about "a little leaven"?________________

22. What miracle did Elisha work to save three kings?________________

23. What is the beginning of the sentence which ends "________ in the beauty of holiness"?________________

24. What king of Tyre was Solomon's great friend?________________

25. What example of just retribution is in the Book of Esther? ________________

26. What did Paul say about "godliness with contentment"?________________

27. Who were thrown into the fiery furnace, and why?________________

28. Who were the Pharisees?________________

29. Finish the quotation: "It is good for a man that he bear______." ________________

30. Who used the metaphor of an axe laid at the roots of trees? ________________

31. What is said in Hebrews about Christ's temptation and sinlessness? ________________

32. What is the Second Commandment, in brief?________________

SERIES X

1. Where was Samuel's home?------------------------------
2. To whom did Christ announce the necessity for a new birth?--
3. When and by whom was the exhortation spoken, "Be strong, and quit yourselves like men"?------------------------------
4. Whom did John the Baptist urge to "bring forth fruits meet for repentence"?------------------------------
5. Quote exactly the angels' Christmas song at Bethlehem.-------

----
6. What Old Testament leader was a stanch defender of the Sabbath? ------------------------------
7. Where and what was Solomon's Porch?--------------------
8. Who was the first murderer?------------------------------
9. How many songs did Solomon write?----------------------
10. Complete the proverb, "Trust in the Lord with all thine heart ------------." ------------------------------
11. How did Christ heal the man with a withered hand?----------

----
12. Who said "Silver and gold have I none; but such as I have give I thee," and to whom did he say it?--------------------
13. Finish the verse: "When we were yet without strength,------."

----
14. Of what did God make the rainbow a token?-----------------
15. What does God's name, "Jehovah," mean?------------------
16. Complete Paul's sentence: "We are laborers---------."--------

33. What two comparisons did Christ use to show that the new and old cannot be closely joined together?____________________
34. In what connection did Christ say that not the healthy but the sick need a physician?____________________________________
35. How did James define religion?____________________________________
36. Who were the Sadducees?______________________________________
37. Locate the phrase, "Good tidings of great joy."_________________
38. Finish the Beautitude: "Blessed are the poor in spirit__________."
____
39. What church, named in the Revelation, had left its first love?
____
40. Locate the reference, in a single verse, to "the cornet, flute, harp, sackbut, psaltery, dulcimer, and all kinds of music."____
____
41. To whom did God say, "Whoso sheddeth man's blood, by man shall his blood be shed"?_____________________________________
42. To whom did the risen Christ show himself first?______________
43. Whose preaching is condensed into the words, "Repent ye: for the kingdom of heaven is at hand"?___________________________
44. Where was Moses bidden to take off his shoes?_________________
____
45. What man, when healed by Christ, was bidden to rise, take up his bed, and go home?____
46. What is the greatest of all uses to which a manger was ever put? ____
47. What was a scapegoat?____
48. What Jewish ruler visited Jesus by night?_____________________
49. Where did the prophet Amos live?______________________________
50. To whom did Moses say, "Come thou with us, and we will do thee good"?____

17. Of what ancient hero is it said that "he was a mighty hunter before the Lord"?________________________

18. Finish the message of the risen Christ to the church of Smyrna: "Be thou faithful unto death__________."__________

19. How does the Bible describe the fruitfulness of Canaan?______
____

20. Who was it that "kept all these things and pondered them in her heart"? ________________________

21. To what did Christ compare the coming of the Holy Spirit?___
____

22. What was the Day of Atonement?________________________

23. When Noah got drunk, what two sons of his walked backward so as not to see his disgrace, and spread a garment over him?
____

24. What was Taberah?________________________

25. Who were the elders of the Israelites?________________________

26. How many Bible passages did the Jews place in the compartments of their phylacteries?________________________

27. What general was encouraged by Deborah?________________

28. What saintly man in the temple blessed the infant Jesus?_____
____

29. On what occasion did Moses say, "Would God that all the Lord's people were prophets"? ________________________

30. What was the origin of the saying, "Is Saul also among the prophets?" ________________________

31. What did Hiram supply for the temple of Solomon?_________
____

32. For what is the tower of Babel famed?________________________

33. To what did Christ compare the brazen serpent?____________
____

34. What did Elisha do for the widow whose two sons were likely to be taken as bondmen for debt?________________________

____

35. With what event is "the sound of going in the tops of the mulberry trees" connected?________________________

____

36. What three signs of his divine mission did the Lord give Moses? ____

37. Who spoke the *Nunc dimittis?*

____

38. What man "went to seek his father's asses and found a kingdom"? ____

39. Finish the quotation, "Weeping may endure for a night, but ____________." ____

40. Complete the Beatitude: "Blessed are they which are persecuted for righteousness sake__________."__________________

41. How did Christ justify his disciples' act in plucking ears of grain on the Sabbath and eating them?__________________

42. What is the rest of the command in Ecclesiastes, "When thou vowest a vow unto God__________"? ______________________

43. When did Christ cook a meal for his disciples?______________

44. What is the Eighth Commandment?______________________

45. What is the greatest verse in the Bible?____________________

46. Where was Idumea?____________________________________

47. What evil deed was done by Achan?______________________

48. Who was Annas?______________________________________

49. "Lying lips are an abomination to the Lord__________"—what is the rest of the proverb?______________________________

50. What is the first part of Christ's saying which ends:"________ and not man for the Sabbath"?____________________________

SERIES XI

1. Who was Abraham's (Abram's) wife?____________________
2. Who said, "Who hath made man's mouth?" and to whom, and on what occasion?____________________________________
3. What leader fell off a seat and broke his neck?____________
4. What was the Jewish law regarding the eating of blood?_____
5. What is the beginning of the verse that ends: "but that the world through him might be saved"?____________________
6. Who asked, "Am I my brother's keeper?"_________________
7. What cities were in Samuel's judicial circuit?______________
8. What occurred after the coming of the great flock of quails at Kibroth-hattaavah in the wilderness?____________________
9. Where in the Bible is the finest account of wisdom?__________
10. What were the Israelites commanded to do to the Hittites, Girgashites, Amorites, Canaanites, Perizzites, Hivites, and Jebusites? ____
11. What Hebrew king was learned in botany and zoölogy?______
12. Who was Lot?____
13. At what city was Joshua's army defeated, afterwards capturing it by an ambush?_________________________________
14. How was Saul indicated as the king?______________________
15. What does the Jewish feast of Purim celebrate?______________
16. Who slew Sisera, and in what way?_______________________

17. Where did Job live?____
18. When Browning wrote, "Our times are in his hand," whom was he quoting?____
19. What were the dimensions of Solomon's temple?____________
____
20. What was Decapolis?____
21. Who were called by Christ "Boanerges," "sons of thunder"?__
____
22. Where were Mounts Ebal and Gerizim, and what did Joshua do there?____
23. Which one of the twelve disciples was not from Galilee but from Judah?____
24. Who was Emperor of Rome during Christ's ministry?________
25. What physical characteristic of Saul distinguished him?______
26. In Isaiah's very beautiful parable beginning, "My beloved hath a vineyard in a very fruitful hill," what does the vineyard symbolize? ____
27. Preaching on the seashore, what device did Christ use to avoid the pressure of the crowd?__________________________________
28. What kindness was shown Elisha by a Shunammite woman?
____
29. Why at one time did Christ's friends try to lay hold on him?
____
30. What wicked king of Judah was punished by being carried to Babylon, where he repented, and was restored to Jerusalem?
____
31. Who was Governor of Judæa during Christ's ministry?_______
32. Why did David's wife Michal "despise him in her heart"?____
____

33. Name the twelve apostles________________________________
____

34. Who ruled over Galilee during Christ's ministry, and what was his title?________________________________

35. What does the proverb say of "hope deferred"?____________

36. What does the term, "beyond Jordan," mean?______________

37. When Ecclesiastes says that "the king himself is served by the field," what does he mean?________________________

38. Why was Christ taken to Jerusalem at the age of twelve?_____
____

39. What is the Ninth Commandment?______________________

40. When did Christ quote Deut. 8: 3: "Man shall not live by bread alone"? ____

41. Christ said that men loved darkness rather than light; why?___
____

42. Who made a fourth with the three Hebrews in the fiery furnace? ____

43. For what is Ænon remembered?_________________________

44. What is the theme of the song of Deborah and Barak?________
____

45. Complete Peter's tribute to Christ, "There is none other name under heaven given among men__________________________."

46. Which Herod cast John the Baptist into prison, and why?_____
____

47. Finish Paul's sentence, "While we were yet sinners, ________."

48. What does the proverb say of one "that spareth his rod"?_____
____

49. What New Testament preacher called his hearers "vipers"?___

50. To whom did Christ say, "Follow me, and I will make you fishers of men"?__________________________________

SERIES XII

1. Who was appointed spokesman for Moses?________________
2. What is "that ancient river, the river Kishon," and what happened there? ________________
3. What is the meaning of Ichabod?________________
4. What were Christ's three temptations in the wilderness?______ ________________
5. What was Abraham's boyhood home?________________
6. When did Christ say, "Wist ye not that I must be about my Father's business"?________________
7. Who said, "My punishment is greater than I can bear"?______
8. What was the noble answer of John the Baptist when he was told of the very great popularity of Jesus?________________ ________________
9. Where was Haran, and with what Bible event is it associated? ________________
10. Finish the proverb: "The path of the just is as the shining light." ________________
11. How many Beatitudes did Christ pronounce?________________
12. In Christ's parable, what happened to the seeds that fell among thorns? ________________
13. Who was Herodias?________________
14. From which of the sons of Adam was Joseph of Nazareth descended? ________________
15. "Let my people go"—said when and to whom?________________ ________________

16. Who gave the command, "He that hath two coats, let him impart to him that hath none"?------------------------------

17. On what occasion did Christ say, "No prophet is accepted in his own country"?--

18. Who first said, "Man doth not live by bread only, but by every word that proceedeth out of the mouth of the Lord"?---------

19. What and where was Samaria?----------------------------

20. How old was Christ when he entered on his ministry?---------

21. Besides his immediate family, whom did Abraham take with him to Canaan?--

22. Of what two untaught men, when they preached ably, was it said, "They have been with Jesus"?------------------------

23. In picturing the coming Christ, what did John the Baptist say would be in his hand?-----------------------------------

24. Why did the Jews "have no dealings with the Samaritans" (John 4: 9)?--

25. From what prophet did Jesus read in the synagogue at Nazareth? --

26. Whence came the phrase, "Bricks without straw"?----------

27. Finish the quotation: "Let your light so shine before men-----"

----

28. What did Christ say was the unpardonable sin?--------------

29. What was Eschol?--

30. What is a parable?--------------------------------------

31. What is the First Commandment?------------------------

32. In Christ's parable, what happened to the seeds that fell by the wayside? --

33. Where was Jacob's well?--------------------------------

34. What was the first recorded act of Abraham in Canaan?------

----

35. Who did Christ say were the same to him as his mother, his sister, and his brother?____

36. What people came to Joshua dressed in old clothes and with mouldy bread and pretended that they had come from a very distant place?____

37. What was the "sixth hour" in New Testament times?_________

38. Where in the Bible did a rod swallow up other rods?_________

39. By what saying did Christ answer the charge that Satan worked miracles through him?____

____

40. Who was the greatest of the Judges, except Samuel?__________

41. What kindly provision for the poor had the Jews in their harvesting? ____

42. What eight classes of persons did Christ pronounce blessed?__

____

43. What was the origin of the phrase, "hewers of wood and drawers of water"?____

44. To what classes did Christ say he came to minister?__________

____

45. Why did Abraham go from Canaan to Egypt?_______________

____

46. Of whose preaching is it said, "His word was with power"?___

47. In Christ's parable, what happened to the seeds that fell on stony ground?____

48. Why did Miriam become a leper, for a time?_______________

____

49. In the Sermon on the Mount to what two things did Christ compare Christians?____

50. Name the ten plagues of Egypt____________________________

____

SERIES XIII

1. What is the chief illustration of a hardened heart in the Bible?
----
2. What is the refrain of Psalm 136, ending each of its twenty-six verses? --
3. Who gave the advice, "Be content with your wages," and to whom did he give it? --
4. Finish the proverb: "Keep thy heart with all diligence; for---"
----
5. Where did the Amalekites live? ------------------------------
6. Who said, "Is not this great Babylon, that I have built?" ------
----
7. Who was Seth? ---
8. What were the five great cities of the Philistines? -----------
----
9. Complete the Beatitude: "Blessed are the peacemakers------."
----
10. Who was Abraham's father?-----------------------------------
11. In Christ's parable, what happened to the seeds that fell on the good ground?--
12. Against what nation did Gideon fight?----------------------
13. What is the Seventh Commandment?--------------------------
14. By what was Jonah swallowed up?--------------------------
15. What did Christ say about swearing?------------------------
16. What falsehood is recorded of Abraham?-------------------
----

17. What is the command of "the second mile"?________________
____
18. On what occasion was the answer given, "We cannot but speak the things which we have seen and heard"?________________
____
19. Which Psalm has some word meaning God's law in every one of its 176 verses?________________________________
20. Which of Christ's parables speaks of "the cares of this world, and the deceitfulness of riches"?________________________
21. What two disciples ran to the tomb on Easter morning? Which arrived first, and which entered first?____________________
22. What was Lot's choice of an abiding place?________________
____
23. What is the first act recorded of Barnabas?________________
____
24. What is Christ's saying about measures?__________________
____
25. What three prophets belong to the period of the return from exile? ____
26. Locate the sentence, "Launch out into the deep."______________
27. What great king ate grass like an ox?____________________
28. On what occasion was a well of water promised, "springing up into everlasting life"?____________________________
29. Where did Abraham live in Canaan?______________________
30. Finish Paul's sentence: "Where sin abounded________."______
31. Who of the twelve spies gave a brave and encouraging report?
____
32. Who was Gehazi?____
33. Complete the proverb: "There is a way which seemeth right unto a man but______."________________________________

34. What were the prescriptions for the passover lamb?---------

----

35. What does "Barnabas" mean?------------------------------

36. What was Christ's command of perfection?-----------------

37. Finish the sentence: "God is a Spirit: and they that worship him must------------." ---------------------------------------

38. Why did the Lord forbid the Israelites (all but two) to enter Canaan? --

39. Finish the sentence: "Many sorrows shall be to the wicked: but --."

40. How were the walls of the temple finished within?----------

----

41. What did Job say when he learned of the death of all his dear ones and the loss of all his goods?--------------------------

42. In what manner were the Jews to eat the passover lamb?-----

----

43. What are the "Songs of Ascents" or "Degrees"?--------------

----

44. Who was Asaph?---

----

45. Where was Saul's home?----------------------------------

46. What was the Jewish rule about paying wages?--------------

----

47. Who are "sons" or "children" of Belial?--------------------

----

48. Why were the Israelites bidden to wander forty years in the wilderness? --

49. Who said, and when: "Depart from me, for I am a sinful man, O Lord"?---

50. Who were the Anakim?------------------------------------

SERIES XIV

1. Where were Sodom and Gomorrah?______________________
2. To what parts of the houses was the blood of the passover lamb applied? ______________________________________
3. What was done to the man who gathered sticks on the Sabbath? ____
4. What was the first name of Barnabas?____________________
5. With what words did Christ forbid vainglory in almsgiving?__

____
6. What was the significance of the fringe and the blue ribbon on the borders of Hebrew garments?_________________________
7. With what parable in three phrases did Christ picture the slow and orderly growth of the kingdom of God?_______________
8. What king seized Lot and his goods?_____________________
9. To what seed did Christ compare his kingdom in its little beginnings? _____________________________________
10. To what fisherman did Christ say, "From henceforth thou shalt catch men"?_________________________________
11. What other name has the passover?_______________________
12. Who said, "Lord, if thou wilt, thou canst make me clean"?____

____
13. With what words did Christ forbid vainglorious prayers?_____
14. What reason did the Lord give for bestowing Canaan on the Israelites? ___________________________________
15. Who was let down through a hole in a roof and so brought before Jesus?_____________________________________

16. To what woman did Jesus, when she spoke of the Messiah, declare, "I that speak unto thee am he"?______________________
17. Complete this quotation: "The world passeth away, and the lust thereof; but_______________________________________."
18. What did Christ say his "meat" was?______________________
19. How did Ananias become a term of reproach?_______________
20. What is the Third Commandment?__________________________
21. To what porch of the temple did the early Christians often resort? ____
22. For whom did an angel draw fire from a rock which consumed a meal prepared for him?_____________________________
23. What is said of Peter's shadow?_________________________
24. Who was Melchizedek?____________________________________
25. On what occasion did twelve prisoners escape the Sanhedrin? ____
26. The people of what town were threatened by the Ammonites with the loss of their right eyes, and who saved them?_______ ____
27. Complete the command in Leviticus, "Ye shall keep my sabbaths, and ____."
28. Who said, "We ought to obey God rather than men," and on what occasion?____
29. Why did the sun and moon stand still at the command of Joshua? ____
30. Who was Sapphira?_______________________________________ ____
31. How did the passover come to be so called?_______________ ____
32. Where was Christ when he spoke of the white harvest fields?__ ____

33. What command in Leviticus was quoted in the New Testament summary of the law?____
34. What did Paul say is the wages of sin?__________________________
35. Complete the call to prayer in Hebrews: "Let us therefore come boldly unto the throne of grace, that____________________."
36. What is the origin of the phrase, "spoiling the Egyptians"?___ ____
37. What does James call "the royal law"?______________________ ____
38. Paul said that all the law was fulfilled in one word; what "word"? ____
39. What is the story of Joshua and the five kings?________________
40. Which of Paul's letters was a circular letter to a number of churches? ____
41. Leviticus bids the Jews love as themselves the strangers dwelling among them; why?____
42. Where in the Bible is the account of the "white stone, and in the stone a new name written"?______________________________________
43. Who testified, "This is indeed the Christ, the Saviour of the world"? ____
44. Where was Saul made king the second time?____________________
45. In what two Gospels is the Lord's Prayer found?________________
46. What law had the Israelites regarding honesty in trade?______ ____
47. Finish the sentence: "Where your treasure is__________________."
48. Of what building are we told that no sound of hammer nor axe nor any other iron tool was heard in the building of it?____ ____
49. Who wrote, "Faith without works is dead"?____________________
50. How did Paul characterize the love of money?__________________

SERIES XV

1. Where was Barnabas born?------------------------------
2. Of whom was it said, "He believed in the Lord; and he counteth it to him for righteousness"?------------------------
3. What king saw the writing on the wall?--------------------
4. Of what wood was the ark of the covenant made?-----------
5. Finish the Beatitude: "Blessed are the merciful."------------
6. How does the Psalm begin which describes the impossibility of running away from God?------------------------------
7. In what Book of the Bible is "a horror of great darkness" mentioned? ---------------------------------------
8. What Old Testament prophet wrote, "The just shall live by his faith," and what New Testament writer insisted on the same doctrine? ------------------------------------
9. What did Haggai say became of the wages the people earned? --
10. How was Molech worshipped? ---------------------------
11. What are the two masters that Christ said no man can serve at at the same time?------------------------------------
12. Who were Korah, Dathan, and Abiram? --------------------
13. What wonderful discourse is reported in John 14, 15, and 16? --
14. To what Bible character did God give the sign of a smoking furnace and a burning lamp passing between the pieces of his sacrifice? ------------------------------------
15. Warning against worry, what did Christ say? ("Sufficient----------------.") ------------------------------------

16. On what occasion did Christ say, "Peace, be still"?___________
17. Finish this sentence from the description of the New Jerusalem: "The glory of God did lighten it, and________." _________
18. Where was the country of the Gadarenes?_________________
19. What was the first rendezvous of the Israelites as they were leaving Egypt? ____
20. What became of the devil whose name was Legion?__________
____
21. What Judge began his work by throwing down the altar of Baal? ____
22. What is the origin of the phrase, "Clothed, and in his right mind"? ____
23. How long were the Israelites in Egypt?___________________
24. What disciple made a great feast to celebrate his conversion?
____
25. Who chose the first king of Israel?______________________
26. On what occasion did Christ ask, "Is it lawful on the Sabbath days to do good, or do evil?"____________________________
27. How high were the golden cherubim of the Most Holy Place?
____
28. What was probably Nathanael's other name? ______________
____
29. How does Luke's report of the Sermon on the Mount differ from Matthew's? _______________________________________
30. How did Elisha repay the kindness of the Shunammite woman?
____
31. What was Christ's second miracle in Galilee? _____________
____
32. Who said, falsely, "All that a man hath will he give for his life"? ____

33. Where is the Pool of Bethesda? ____________________________
34. Who said, "I dwell among mine own people"? _____________
35. Which of the disciples would seem to have had the most names? ____
36. Who was Zadok? ______________________________________
37. Whom did Christ heal at the Pool of Bethesda? ____________ ____
38. Who did Christ say was "a burning and a shining light"? ____ ____
39. What kind of nation did the Psalmist call "blessed"? ________ ____
40. How large was the lad's lunch which Christ made to feed five thousand persons? _____________________________________
41. Finish the proverb: "Righteousness exalteth a nation: but___." ____
42. How did Christ illustrate the principle of thrift? ___________ ____
43. On what occasion did Christ say, "My Father worketh hitherto, and I work"? ____
44. "When goods increase," says Ecclesiastes; how is the sentence finished? ____
45. Who was Gamaliel? ___________________________________
46. What led to the appointing of the first deacons? ___________ ____
47. About how large was an ephah? _________________________
48. Name the first deacons. ______________________________
49. Finish Jeremiah's question: "Can the Ethiopian change his skin?" ____
50. How much was left after Christ fed the five thousand with five cakes and two small fishes? ___________________________

SERIES XVI

1. To what body does the New Testament refer under the name of "the council"? ____________
2. Who was Ishmael's mother? ____________
3. What is the longest prayer reported in the New Testament? ____________
4. What was the significance of the change of name from Abram to Abraham? ____________
5. What did Stephen say about the learning of Moses? ____________
6. Where is the command, "An eye for an eye, a tooth for a tooth," to be found? ____________
7. What is the character of "an Ishmael"? ____________
8. Whom did Paul urge to "fight the good fight of faith"? ____________
9. Why was Aaron's rod that budded laid up in the Holy of Holies? ____________
10. How many members had the Sanhedrin? ____________
11. From what two mountains were blessings and curses proclaimed? ____________
12. How was Abraham's hospitality to three strangers rewarded? ____________
13. What is described in Hebrews as "an anchor of the soul, both sure and stedfast"? ____________
14. Why, in the exodus, did not the Israelites go by the straight and short northern route to Canaan? ____________

15. What portion of Canaan was assigned to Caleb as a reward of his faith? ________
16. Of whom is it said that at his trial his face was as that of an angel? ________
17. What name was given to Gideon? ________
18. Of what was James speaking when he wrote, "Behold, how great a matter a little fire kindleth!"? ________
19. What token did Samuel obtain to prove to the people that God was with him? ________
20. How long was Solomon in building the temple? ________
21. Into what three periods is the life of Moses divided? ________
22. Who asked, "Is anything too hard for the Lord"? ________
23. What wife of Abraham fled to the wilderness? ________
24. What two said that God "dwelleth not in temples made with hands"? ________
25. Whose bones did Moses take with him in the exodus from Egypt? ________
26. By what test was Gideon assured that God was with him? ________
27. Which of the seven churches of Asia had a name to be living but was dead? ________
28. On what occasion did the prophet Nathan make a mistake? ________
29. Who were Job's three friends who came to comfort him? ________
30. Who was the first Christian martyr, and how was he killed? ________
31. Finish the verse: "The Lord is nigh unto them that are of a broken heart; and ________." ________

32. How long was Solomon in building his palace? ______________
33. Who are represented as crying: "Holy, holy, holy, is the Lord of hosts"? ______________
34. What supernatural guidance had the Israelites in the exodus and the wilderness wanderings? ______________
35. What is the point of Christ's little parable of the mote and the beam? ______________
36. What did Elisha do with the poisonous pottage? ______________
37. Who were the "rulers of the synagogue"? ______________
38. What did Moses say when the people seemed caught in a trap in their escape from Egypt? ______________
39. Finish Job's sentence, referring to death: "There the wicked cease from troubling; and ____________." ______________
40. To what does Ecclesiastes compare the laughter of a fool? ______________
41. How many men did Elisha feed with twenty barley cakes? ______________
42. Finish the Beatitude, "Blessed are they that mourn." ______________
43. Who gave a synagogue to the Jews of Capernaum? ______________
44. How did Stephen imitate Christ in his death? ______________
45. When did the Jews try to make Jesus a king? ______________
46. Quote the proverb about a soft answer. ______________
47. Who is mentioned as present at the stoning of Stephen? ______________
48. Complete the quotation: "To be carnally minded is death; but ______________." ______________
49. What may be said to be Paul's most hopeful saying? ______________
50. What promise and command did Moses give his people when they seemed hemmed in by the pursuing Egyptians? ______________

SERIES XVII

1. Complete Paul's question, "If God be for us................."
2. How does the Book of Proverbs end? ....
3. How were the Levites supported? ....
4. What is the oft-quoted sentence in Ecclesiastes about "the former days"? ....
5. Who was Naaman? ....
6. Quote Paul's "other foundation" verse. ....
7. Besides Solomon, who wrote sections of the Book of Proverbs? ....
8. What was the Hebrew law of releases? ....
9. Who was consecrated for his work by a live coal from the altar? ....
10. Who is referred to in Paul's sentence, "He is our peace"? ....
11. Finish the quotation, "Many are the afflictions of the righteous: but ...."
12. Who is the famous "little maid" of the Old Testament? ....
13. Where in the Bible is the motto that is on the Independence Bell, "Proclaim liberty," etc.? ....
14. Who wrote, "I know whom I have believed," and to whom was he writing? ....
15. What proverb about sour grapes is quoted by Ezekiel in order to disprove it? ....
16. When a Hebrew bondservant chose perpetual servitude, what ceremony bound him to it? ....

17. What is the rest of the proverb, "The eyes of the Lord are in every place............"? ....
18. Finish the Beatitude: "Blessed are they which do hunger and thirst after righteousness..............." ....
19. Where in the Bible is the expression, "Weighed in the balances, and found wanting"? ....
20. What was the law regarding the release of Hebrew bondservants? ....
21. What became of the thirty pieces of silver for which Judas betrayed Christ? ....
22. What reason did James give for failures to obtain answers to prayer? ....
23. In whose reign was the long-lost Book of the Law discovered, and by whom? ....
24. What was the purpose of the cities of refuge? ....
25. Complete Jeremiah's estimate: "The heart is deceitful above all things, and............." ....
26. What was the "lukewarm" church of the Revelation? ....
27. In what address are the words about casting pearls before swine? ....
28. Name the six cities of refuge. ....
29. What is wrong with a reference to "the straight and narrow way"? ....
30. What was the length of Solomon's palace? ....
31. To what church in the Revelation is it said: "Thou hast a little strength, and hast kept my word, and hast not denied my name"? ....
32. Who was Jaïrus? ....
33. How did King Saul disobey God? ....
34. Finish this sentence from Ezekiel: "The soul that sinneth....."

35. Who asked, "Shall not the Judge of all the earth do right"?---

----

36. Why did Christ say of the Capernaum centurion that he had not found so great faith as his among the Jews? ------------

----

37. What general won a great victory through cutting his army down from 32,000 to 300? ----------------------------------

38. What three disciples were admitted to the raising from the dead of the daughter of Jaïrus? ---------------------------

39. Who made the bronze or copper work for Solomon's temple?

----

40. What is the remainder of the proverb, "Better is a dinner of herbs where love is-------------"? -----------------------

41. Who said, "Speak unto the children of Israel, that they go forward," and to whom did he say it? ---------------------

42. Where is Nain? --

43. When did Christ say to his disciples, "It is I; be not afraid"?

----

44. What law had the Jews for resting their fields? -----------

----

45. Who wrote, "In thy light shall we see light"? --------------

46. To whom did Christ say, "Talitha cumi"? -----------------

47. What was the year of jubilee? --------------------------

----

48. What were the names of the two pillars of the porch of Solomon's temple? --

----

49. To whom did Christ say, "Young man, I say unto thee, Arise"?

----

50. For what cities did Abraham plead with God? -------------

SERIES XVIII

1. In connection with what miracle did Christ say, "Labor not for the meat which perisheth"? ______________________________
2. What portion of the Red Sea did Moses and his people cross? ______________________________
3. How many times a year were Jews required to visit the temple in Jerusalem? ______________________________
4. Finish the quotation from Hebrews: "He is able to save them to the uttermost that come unto God by him, seeing__________."
5. What were the Mosaic laws regarding justice? ______________
6. Where and why was the altar, Ed, erected? ______________ ______________________________
7. Who wrote a psalm to celebrate the passage of the Red Sea? ______________________________
8. What is the origin of the famous phrase, "The sword of the Lord and of Gideon"? ______________________________
9. What did Christ say is "the work of God"? ______________
10. What was placed in the ark of the covenant? ______________
11. Who led the dances of the women after the passage of the Red Sea? ______________________________
12. On what occasion was the angel seen standing between heaven and earth, having a drawn sword in his hand stretched over Jerusalem? ______________________________
13. Complete the sentence from James: "God resisteth the proud, but ___________." ______________________________
14. In connection with the feeding of the five thousand, what name did Christ give himself? ______________________________

15. What did Jonathan say to his armorbearer before the two attacked the Philistine army? ____________________

16. What rivers did Naaman deem better than the Jordan, if he were to be healed of leprosy by bathing? ____________________

17. During Saul's persecution of the Jerusalem Christians, which deacon went to Samaria and preached there, working miracles? ____________________

18. What is the most extended report of a prayer in the Old Testament? ____________________

19. What happened at the waters of Marah? ____________________

20. Who was David's strongest general? ____________________

21. Where did Simon the sorcerer live, and who converted him?
____

22. Where lived the giant who had six fingers on each hand and six toes on each foot? ____________________

23. As Gideon's three hundred attacked the Midianites, what means did they use to produce terror? ____________________

24. What was Meribah ("the water of Meribah")? ____________________

25. Why did Peter rebuke Simon of Samaria? ____________________

26. Finish Job's sentence, "Man is born unto trouble, as__________."

27. Who used the expression, "The gall of bitterness and the bond of iniquity"; and in what connection? ____________________

28. Finish the sentence: "A little that a righteous man hath______."

29. For what do we remember Elim? ____________________

30. How did Jonathan and his armorbearer put to flight the Philistines at Michmash? ____________________

31. What is the first part of Paul's sentence ending "through him that loved us"? ____________________

32. Where did Kipling get the title of his book, "Many Inventions"? ____________________

33. What was the ancient Hebrew law about land ownership? ---
----
34. Who said that a Christian is the temple of God, his Spirit dwelling in him? ----------------------------------
35. Where is the prophecy of the birth of Immanuel from a virgin? --
36. What is the rest of the proverb, "Pride goeth before destruction"? --------------------------------------
37. Who called himself "less than the least of all saints," and why?
38. Whom did Paul bid to "endure hardness, as a good soldier of Jesus Christ"? ----------------------------------
39. Who was Maher-shalal-hashbaz? ---------------------------
40. What was the Hebrew law about taking interest? -----------
----
41. What prophet forbade the people of Jerusalem to carry burdens on the Sabbath? ------------------------------
42. Where in the Bible is the picture of Christ standing at the door and knocking? ----------------------------------
43. What prophet was thrown into a lions' den, and why? --------
44. Where did Miriam die? -----------------------------------
45. In what prophetic Book is the command, "Prepare to meet thy God"? --
46. Why was Zoar ("smallness") so called? -------------------
47. What great city repented at the preaching of Jonah? ---------
----
48. How did Moses sin in drawing water out of a rock? ---------
49. What prophet cried, "Woe to him that giveth his neighbor drink!"? ---------------------------------------
50. Why did Lot's wife become a pillar of salt? -----------------
----

SERIES XIX

1. Who prophesied concerning "the desire of all nations"? -----
2. Who spoke of the impossibility of gathering "grapes of thorns, or figs of thistles"? --
3. With what event do you associate the words, "It is hard for thee to kick against the pricks"? --------------------------
4. What is the meaning of "the Lord of Sabaoth"? ------------
5. Where did Christ say, "A prophet is not without honor, but in his own country"? --
6. Who wrote the famous formula, "One Lord, one faith, one baptism"? --
7. Whom did Paul exhort to be "a workman that needeth not to be ashamed"? ---
8. How did Christ provide for co-operation among disciples? ---
   ----
9. What was in the Holy Place of Solomon's temple? ----------
   ----
10. Who said, "By their fruits ye shall know them"? -----------
11. What was kept in the Most Holy Place of the temple? --------
   ----
12. Who was Salome? ---
13. Finish the quotation from James, "Resist the devil----------."
   ----
14. What is signified by the "golden vials full of odors," of Revelation? ---
15. In what connection did Christ say, "Wisdom is justified of all her children"? --

16. What miracle attended the gathering of the manna? ________
____
17. On what occasion did Christ speak the parable of the two debtors? ____
18. To the lands of what king did Abraham go and tell there his second lie? ____________________________________
19. Where did Moses first draw water from a rock? ___________
20. With what parable did Christ close the Sermon on the Mount?
____
21. What was the cause of the long quarrel between the Israelites and their kindred, the Edomites? ______________________
22. What was the law of the Hebrews with regard to witnesses in executions? ____________________________________
23. Who was Simon the Pharisee? __________________________
____
24. How was the Sabbath kept in the matter of the manna? _____
____
____
25. Who was the son of Abraham's old age? __________________
26. Who did Herod Antipas think that Jesus was? ____________
____
27. What did Christ say was "the living bread"? ____________
____
28. Where did Joshua speak his farewell address? ___________
29. Where did Aaron die? _________________________________
30. Who was it said to Christ, "Lord, to whom shall we go? thou hast the words of eternal life"? _____________________
31. What did the manna taste like? _______________________
32. On what occasion and by whom were the words spoken, "Choose you this day whom ye will serve"? ______________

33. On what occasion did Christ say, "If any man thirst, let him come unto me, and drink"? ______________________
34. What son of Abraham's was saved by a miraculous well of water in the wilderness? ______________________
35. With what tribe did the Israelites fight at Rephidim? ________
36. Who said of Christ, "Never man spake like this man"? ______ ______________________
37. Where were the bones of Joseph buried? ______________
38. Locate the phrase, "Faint, yet pursuing." ______________ ______________________
39. For what reason was Saul about to kill Jonathan? __________ ______________________
40. What member of the Sanhedrin spoke for justice when the other members were seeking to arrest Jesus? ______________
41. What king of what nation did Saul spare, contrary to God's command? ______________________
42. Who succeeded Aaron as high priest? ______________________
43. Under what queen did the Ethiopian treasurer serve? ________
44. How did Moses aid in the battle of Rephidim, and who helped him? ______________________
45. What king of Judah saw his sons slain and then was himself blinded by his enemies? ______________________
46. What prophet was the Ethiopian treasurer reading, and what apostle explained the passage to him? ______________________
47. Who said, "To obey is better than sacrifice," and to whom did he say it? ______________________
48. Who gave to Jehovah the title, "The Strength of Israel"? _____
49. To what great city in Syria did Saul seek to extend his persecutions? ______________________
50. What was the manna? ______________________

SERIES XX

1. Why was Gehazi made a leper? ______________________
2. What is the teaching of Christ's little parable of the candle on the candlestick? ______________________
3. What were the names of Job's three beautiful daughters?_____
____
4. On what occasion did Christ write on the ground? __________
5. What miracle did Christ work in the country of the Gadarenes? ______________________
6. Finish the sentence from the Psalms: "O send out thy light and thy truth:_________." ______________________
7. What was Christ's sentence when the scribes and Pharisees brought him an adulteress? ______________________
8. Explain the phrase, "Bowing in the house of Rimmon." ______
____
9. Complete this saying of Christ's: "I am the____________of the world." ______________________
10. Where was the country of the **Gadarenes?** ______________
11. What is the rest of the proverb, "There is a way that seemeth right unto a man, but___________."? ______________________
12. With what words did Christ declare his perfection? _________
13. What is the rest of the saying in Ecclesiastes: "A living dog is better than _________."? ______________________
14. Distinguish between the two disciples named Ananias. _______
15. Who wrote the wonderful sentence beginning "Unto us a child is born," and containing the many names of God and Christ?
____

16. Name the six Judases of the New Testament. ______________

____

17. What demoniac was possessed by a demon called Legion?___
18. What prophet is remarkable for the numer of object lessons he used? ____
19. Where is the street called Straight? ______________________
20. Who is called "a chosen vessel"? _______________________
21. What prophet was bidden by the Lord, as a sign to the unfaithful people, to marry an unfaithful wife? ______________
22. Who vouched for Saul to the distrustful Christians of Jerusalem? ____
23. What was Paul's home city, and where was it situated? ______

____

24. What prophet characterized the rich as lying on beds of ivory?
25. What man did Jesus free from demons, bidding them enter a herd of swine? ____________________________________
26. Where did Peter cure a palsied man, and what was his name?
27. What two prophets saw the great vision of peace when men should beat their swords into plowshares and their spears into pruninghooks? ____________________________________
28. Where did Dorcas live? ______________________________
29. What two things did Paul say are necessary for salvation? ____

____

30. Complete this sentence from Habakkuk: "The Lord is in his holy temple ____________________________________."
31. What was Dorcas's other name? _________________________
32. Who said to Jesus, "Master, I will follow thee whithersoever thou goest"? _____________________________________
33. Finish Paul's sentence: "The wisdom of this world is________."

____

34. What Epistle was written to "the elect lady and her children"? ______

35. What is Paul's great verse regarding the inspiration of the Scriptures? ______

36. Who wrote "the New Testament addition table," "Add to your faith virtue," etc.? ______

37. On what occasion did Christ say, "The foxes have holes, and the birds of the air have nests; but the Son of man hath not where to lay his head"? ______

38. What is meant when a woman is called "a Dorcas"? ______

39. In what Book is the picture of Death on a pale horse? ______

40. Where is Mount Moriah? ______

41. On what occasion did Christ say, "Let the dead bury their dead"? ______

42. What wise advice did Jethro give Moses? ______

43. What kinds of things did Christ say defile a man? ______

44. What angelic guardianship is promised in one of the Psalms? ______

45. On what occasion was it said of Christ, "He could not be hid"? ______

46. With what words did Peter raise Dorcas from the dead? ______

47. Where did Abraham start to offer up Isaac as a sacrifice? ______

48. What woman obtained from Christ her daughter's health by her quick wit and humility? ______

49. Who was Rabshakeh? ______

50. Out of what woman did Christ cast seven devils? ______

SERIES XXI

1. For what king did a sundial shadow move ten degrees backward as a sign of his extended life, and what prophet announced the sign? --
2. Who were the Rechabites? ------------------------------
3. What did Pilate's wife do during the trial of Christ? ----------
4. What hero, when asked to rule over Israel, said, "I will not rule over you: neither shall my son rule over you: the Lord shall rule over you"? ------------------------------------
5. On what occasion did the Lord say to Samuel: "Man looketh on the outward appearance, but the Lord looketh on the heart"? --
6. Who was Amaziah? --
7. With whom did Peter lodge in Joppa? ----------------------
8. Where was Ophir, from which Solomon obtained gold? ------
9. What is illustrated by Christ's parable of the shepherd who left ninety-nine sheep in order to seek one that was lost? ----
10. What was David's introduction to Saul? --------------------
11. Finish the quotation from Paul: "The foundation of God standeth sure, having this seal, -------------------------------."
12. What prophet made a borrowed axe-head swim to the surface when it fell into the water? ------------------------------
13. What chapter of what Book lists the heroes of faith? --------
14. In what Book is the important prophecy of the Prophet that God would raise up like Moses? ------------------------------
15. What miracle showed that Christ's work cost him something?

----

16. What were the colors and ornamentation of the veil between the Holy Place and the Most Holy Place? ____________________
17. Finish the quotation: "If any man will come after me, let him deny himself______________." ______________________________
18. To whom was it said, "What God hath cleansed, that call not thou common," and on what occasion? ______________________
19. Complete Paul's sentence: "We then that are strong ought to bear the infirmities of the weak, and______________." __________
20. Finish the quotation from Romans, "Whosoever shall call upon the name of the Lord ______________________________."
21. Of what ruler is it said that he desired to see Jesus?__________
22. Where in the Bible is the phrase, "The pen of a ready writer"? ____
23. When was it necessary for Peter, and when for Paul, to refuse to receive worship? ______________________________
24. After what miracle did the astonished multitude say of Christ, "He doeth all things well"? ______________________________
25. What is the origin of the hymn, "I would not live alway"? ____
26. Finish Paul's great sentence: "All things are yours; whether Paul, or ____."
27. What incidents show that Christ was in the habit of asking a blessing at the table? ______________________________________
28. What prophet was a herdman and also tended sycomore trees?
29. Whom did Christ heal with the word, "Ephphatha" ("Be opened")? ____
30. Where in the Bible is the sentence: "He that is slow to anger is better than the mighty; and he that ruleth his spirit than he that taketh a city"? ______________________________________
31. Of whom is it written, "He being dead yet speaketh," and in what Book? ____

32. What prophecy is marked by a series of eight great visions?
----
33. Finish James's sentence: "Draw nigh to God, and___________."
34. Who was Phebe? ______________________________________
35. Complete Paul's sentence, "The letter killeth, but__________,"
36. Where is the prophecy that the Messiah was to be born in Bethlehem? ______________________________________
37. What Book of the Bible is an emblematic love song? _________
38. Where is the Bible's most wonderful description of the hosts in heaven and their life there? ___________________________
39. How long a sickness had the woman who was healed by touching the hem of Christ's garment? _________________________
40. Where is the Messianic prophecy of the Branch out of the roots of Jesse? ______________________________________
41. What is the origin of the word Gehenna? __________________
42. Who described the devil as a murderer from the beginning, and what was the rest of his description? _________________
43. In what prophet is a most complete description of ancient commerce? ______________________________________
44. Who was Cornelius, and where did he live? ________________
45. Who uttered the prophecy, "A little child shall lead them"? __
46. What are the Hebrew and Greek names of the angel of the bottomless pit? ___________________________________
47. How did Christ state his preëxistence? __________________
48. Who was Tertius? ______________________________________
----
49. Who said, "If the Son shall make you free, ye shall be free indeed," and to whom did he say it? _______________________
50. What is the meaning of the phrase, "The valley of Achor for a door of hope," and in what prophecy is it? _______________

SERIES XXII

1. What is the origin of the saying, "I am no prophet, nor the son of a prophet"? ______________________________
2. When did Christ's hearers take up stones to cast at him?______
3. When was Peter led to perceive that "God is no respecter of persons"? ______________________________
4. Who asked the question, "How shall they hear without a preacher"? ______________________________
5. What substitute was given to Abraham for the sacrifice of Isaac? ______________________________
6. Where is the sentence, "Be still, and know that I am God"? __ ______________________________
7. What prophet was put in the stocks, and uttered a prophecy against the governor who put him there? ________________
8. In what connection did Christ say, "The night cometh, when no man can work"? ______________________________
9. When conversions to Christianity were made in Antioch of Syria, who was sent thither by the church in Jerusalem? _____
10. What was Jehovah-jireh? ______________________________
11. To what Christian leader in Crete did Paul write a letter?____
12. Finish the phrase from Hebrews: "Jesus Christ the same____."
13. Finish the proverb: "A friend loveth at all times, and_______."
14. Where in the Bible is the reference to "the rose of Sharon, and the lily of the valleys"? ______________________________
15. What field did Abraham buy for a burial place, and who were buried there? ______________________________
16. What is Micah's summary of religion? ______________________

17. Whom did Christ heal, saying, "According to your faith be it unto you"? --
18. With what saying did Christ lament the fewness of evangelists? --

----
19. How did Abraham's servant recognize Rebekah as the maiden whom Isaac should marry? ----------------------------
20. What two Simons among the apostles? ----------------------
21. What miracle of Christ's was gradual in its working?--------

----
22. Who said, "I bare you on eagles' wings, and brought you unto myself," and to whom was it said? ----------------------------
23. Fill in the blanks: "Whosoever will save------------: but whosoever will lose-------------shall save it." ------------------
24. In what prophecy is found God's word to Zerubbabel, "Not by might, nor by power, but by my spirit, saith the Lord of hosts"?

----
25. Who was Balak? --
26. Where is the sentence, "A merry heart doeth good like a medicine"? --
27. What prophet in his sorrow cursed the day of his birth?------
28. Who was Balaam? --
29. What was the Jewish law of landmarks? --------------------
30. In what city were the converts urged "that with purpose of heart they would cleave unto the Lord"? --------------------
31. What was done by Abimelech, the son of Gideon? ------------
32. What two great contributions to our religion were made in Antioch? --
33. What is the story of Balaam's ass? --------------------------

----

34. What was the Jewish law for a stubborn and rebellious son?
----
35. What Jerusalem prophet foretold the great famine in the days of Claudius? ----------------------------------
36. What did Paul urge us to present as a living sacrifice? --------
----
37. Who uttered the prophecy of the Star out of Jacob? ----------
----
38. What did Paul say is required in stewards? ----------------
----
39. Who was Jotham? ------------------------------------
40. How tall was Goliath? ---------------------------------
41. Finish the quotation: "God is our refuge and strength,--------."
----
42. Where was Sheba, and for what is its queen famous? ---------
----
43. What is the meaning of "Making the ephah small, and the shekel great"? ---------------------------------
44. Where was Elisha protected against the Syrians by a mountain full of horses and chariots of fire? ------------------------
45. What did Christ say would happen to any man who was ashamed of him? -------------------------------------
46. Who was Solomon's son and successor? -------------------
47. Just before what miracle did Christ say that he was the light of the world? -----------------------------------
48. Who was Sheshbazzar? --------------------------------
49. Who spoke of a daysman, a mediator, between God and man?
----
50. Who said, and when: "Fear not: for they that be with us are more than they that be with them"? ----------------------

SERIES XXIII

1. Who said of Jesus Christ that he "went about doing good"?___
____
2. Finish the quotation: "Faith cometh by hearing, and________."
____
3. Where is the sentence to be found, "I being in the way, the Lord led me"? _______________________________
4. Where is Sharon? ________________________________
5. What prophet said, "Ephraim is joined to idols; let him alone"? ____
6. What did Paul mean when he urged us to "put off the old man" and "put on the new man"? ____________________
7. Who was Rebekah's brother? ________________________
8. What is the proverb that defines the power of the tongue? ____
____
9. Whom did Paul urge to be "instant in season, out of season"?
____
10. Of what mount was it said that whoever touched it should be put to death? _______________________________
11. Where is the sentence: "He brought me to the banqueting house, and his banner over me was love"? ______________
12. Finish the quotation: "He that cometh to God must believe that he is, and____________." _____________________
13. Who was Phinehas? ___________________________
____
14. Who wrote: "Then shall we know, if we follow on to know the Lord"? ___________________________________

15. Who wrote: "Draw nigh to God, and he will draw nigh to you"? ____________________
16. Who were Tola and Jair? ____________________
17. What Book of the Old Testament has only one chapter? ______
18. Finish the shout of the "great voices in heaven": "The kingdoms of this world are become____________." ______________
____
19. Who asked, "Who hath despised the day of small things?" and how did the question fit his times? ____________________
____
20. How many brothers had David? ____________________
21. Christ bade his apostles to be as wise as__________and harmless as____________; fill the blanks. ____________________
22. Where was Dalmanutha? ____________________
23. Who was David's father? ____________________
24. How many Books in the Bible? in the Old Testament? the New Testament? ____________________
25. Christ bade his apostles take no thought how or what they should speak; his advice was for what occasions? __________
____
26. How many wives had Solomon? ____________________
27. Where was Cæsarea Philippi? ____________________
28. Who was the first martyr among the apostles, and who put him to death? ____________________
29. What did Elisha do to the Syrian army which surrounded him at Dothan? ____________________
30. When did Peter rebuke Christ? ____________________
31. Who was Jeroboam? ____________________
32. Quote the verse about God's being a sun and shield. __________
____

33. Who was Jeshua? ________________________________
34. Finish the quotation: "Abhor that which is evil__________."
35. Who was Nebat? ________________________________
36. When did Christ call Peter Satan? ____________________
37. Who asked, "Canst thou by searching find out God?" and whom did he ask? ________________________________
38. Fill out the quotation: "The kingdom of God is not in_______, but in____________." ________________________________
39. Finish the quotation: "This God is our God for ever and ever: he will be__________." ________________________________
40. Who is referred to as "the great dragon, that old serpent," and where is the sentence? ________________________________
41. Where is the pool of Siloam, and what occurred there? _____
____
42. On what occasions did Peter, James, and John fall asleep when they should have kept awake? ____________________
____
43. Who was Keturah? ________________________________
44. What is "the first commandment with promise"? __________
45. What is Paul's advice about anger? ____________________
____
46. When did Peter propose to make three booths? ___________
47. What is to be noted concerning the daughters of Zelophehad?
____
48. Of whom is it said that "he looked for a city which hath foundations, whose builder and maker is God"? ______________
49. Finish the saying, "To him that knoweth to do good, and doeth it not,_________." ________________________________
50. Who spoke of those who go about from one preacher and speaker to another as "having itching ears"? _____________

SERIES XXIV

1. What Book of the Bible is named for a race? ________________
2. Finish this sentence from the description of the New Jerusalem: "God shall wipe away____________." ____________________
3. What did the law decree about muzzling an ox? _____________
4. Who was Elimelech? ____
5. What was a quaternion? ____________________________________
6. Where did David fight Goliath? _____________________________
7. Who was it said of Christ, "To him give all the prophets witness"? ____
8. How was Peter freed from prison? ___________________________
9. What hero was delivered from a lion and a bear? _____________
10. Complete Paul's phrase, "In honor__________________________."
11. What was Millo? ____
12. In what connection did Paul write, "A little leaven leaveneth the whole lump"? ____
13. What king of Syria besieged Samaria in the days of Elisha? _
14. What is the prophetical Book of the New Testament? _________
15. What foolish young king forsook the counsel of the old advisers and followed that of the young counsellors? _____________
16. In what three short sentences did Paul sum up his life? ______ ____
17. Which are the "synoptic Gospels"? __________________________
18. Why did the old men weep when the foundations of the second temple were laid? ____
19. What are the "early" and the "latter" rains? ________________

20. What Book of the Bible was written for "the well beloved Gaius"? ______________________

21. Who said sarcastically, "No doubt but ye are the people, and wisdom shall die with you," and to whom did he say it? _______ ______________________

22. Who wrote the exhortation to "redeem the time" ("buy up the opportunity") ? ______________________

23. Finish the quotation: "Create in me a clean heart, O God; and ______________________."

24. Why was Jacob so called, his name meaning "supplanter"?___ ______________________

25. Why was Esau so called, his name meaning "hairy"? _________

26. What is the first part of the proverb ending "and there is a friend that sticketh closer than a brother"? ________________

27. What is David's penitential psalm? ______________________

28. What command in the law forbids mob rule? ______________ ______________________

29. What command in the law forbids the taking of bribes? ______ ______________________

30. Where is the saying about "the little foxes that spoil the vines"? ______________________

31. What is the chapter of the blessings and the curses? _________

32. What is the origin of "Shibboleth" as meaning a test? ________ ______________________

33. Finish Hosea's prophecy, "They have sown the wind, and they shall____________." ______________________

34. Who were Naomi's sons and their respective wives? __________ ______________________

35. Who said, "The battle is the Lord's" just before a famous combat? ______________________

36. Of what people is it said, "Though thou exalt thyself as the eagle, and though thou set thy nest among the stars, thence will I bring thee down, saith the Lord"? and who wrote it? ______

____

37. Who said, "My little finger shall be thicker than my father's loins"? ______________________________

38. What happy discovery was made by four lepers outside the gate of Samaria? ______________________________

39. What lesson did Christ draw from the sparrows? __________

____

40. On what momentous occasion was the cry raised, "To your tents, O Israel"? ______________________________

41. Finish the quotation: "What shall it profit a man, if_________

____."

42. What caused a long intermission in Zerubbabel's work of rebuilding the temple? ______________________________

43. Who said, "Though he slay me, yet will I trust him"? _______

____

44. On what occasion did Christ say, "All things are possible to him that believeth"? ______________________________

45. Finish the verse: "The fool hath said in his heart,____________

____."

46. Who, according to the proverb, "lendeth unto the Lord"? _____

____

47. How did Christ rebuke the disciples' quarrel over precedence?

____

48. Who was Diotrephes? ______________________________

49. What is "the Epistle of Love"? ______________________________

50. To what part of a fold did Christ compare himself? __________

____

SERIES XXV

1. What do Hosea's words, "I called my son out of Egypt," foretell? ______________________________

2. What was Christ's saying about the hairs of one's head?______

3. What king, because of his pride, was smitten by an angel and died, eaten of worms? ______________________________

4. Who was Jeremiah's secretary for the writing of his prophecies? ______________________________

5. Where is the lovely prophecy of Jerusalem that "the streets of the city shall be full of boys and girls playing in the streets thereof"? ______________________________

6. Who was Demas? ______________________________

7. Of whom is it said that "he endured, as seeing him who is invisible"? ______________________________

8. Who were the first Christian missionaries? ________________

9. Who taught that "the effectual fervent prayer of a righteous man availeth much"? ______________________________

10. In what Book are the beautiful words, referring to Jehovah, "I drew them with cords of a man, with bands of love"? ______

11. What did Christ say about those who should confess him before men and those who should deny him? ________________

12. How many of Peter's Epistles have we? ____________________

13. Who urged Christians to "abstain from all appearance of evil"? ______________________________

14. Christ said, "I came not to send peace, but________."____what?

____

15. Who wrote regarding Christ the beautiful words, "Whom having not seen, ye love"? ______
16. For what did Esau sell his birthright, and to whom? ______
______
17. Who said to Christ, "Lord, I believe; help thou mine unbelief"? ______
18. In whose house in Jerusalem was the prayer meeting held while Peter was in prison? ______
19. How did Isaac prove his peacefulness and patience? ______
20. From what city did the first Christian missionaries set out?
21. Where are the words found, "Blessed are the dead which die in the Lord," etc? ______
22. Locate the words, "As thy days, so shall thy strength be."______
23. Who was Rhoda? ______
24. What did Christ answer when his disciples asked why they could not cure the demoniac boy? ______
25. What and where was Seleucia? ______
26. What was the mercy seat, and why was it so called? ______
27. Where did Peter go on leaving Jerusalem after the angel had freed him from the prison? ______
28. What happening led Christ to say, "If any man desire to be first, the same shall be last of all, and servant of all"? ______
29. What were engraved on the twelve precious stones of the high priest's breastplate? ______
30. Where did the first Christian missionaries do their first work?
______
31. What led Christ to say, "He that is not against us is for us"?
______
32. How did Jacob cheat his aged father and obtain from him the blessing that belonged to Esau? ______

33. What king cut to pieces Jeremiah's prophecies, burning up the roll as he did so? --

34. When a Samaritan village would not receive Christ and his disciples, what did James and John want to do? ------------

35. Who buried Moses, and where? ----------------------------

36. Who were Ibzan, Elon, and Abdon? ------------------------

37. Why did Christ call himself "the good shepherd"? -----------

38. Who went with the first Christian missionaries as their attendant and helper? --

39. How did David arm himself to slay Goliath? ---------------

40. With what words did Christ prophesy Christian union? ------

41. Who was Adoram? --
----

42. Where did Paul always begin his missionary work, though in heathen cities? --

43. Who was Saul's great general? ---------------------------

44. Of what king was it said, "He driveth furiously"? -----------
----

45. With what words did Christ announce his power to bring himself from the grave? ----------------------------------

46. What is Paul's last writing that we possess? ---------------
----

47. Which of Naomi's daughters-in-law turned back to Moab, and which followed her to Bethlehem? -----------------------

48. Where in the Bible is the command to "heap coals of fire" on an enemy's head by doing kindnesses to him? --------------

49. Locate the words, "The eternal God is thy refuge, and underneath are the everlasting arms." --------------------------

50. Paul said, "I am made all things to all men, that------------" what? --

SERIES XXVI

1. Who was Shishak? ____________________
2. What is the very small service for which Christ promised a reward? ____________________
3. What two prophets urged Zerubbabel to complete the rebuilding of the temple? ____________________

____
4. How did Christ describe his yoke and his burden? __________
5. Who complained that "man that is born of woman is of few days, and full of trouble"? ____________________
6. With what saying did Christ insist on the sanctity of marriage?

____
7. Finish the quotation: "Oh that I had wings like a dove!______

____________________"
8. With what saying did Christ exalt little children? __________

____
9. Where is the sentence, "Wine is a mocker," etc.? __________
10. Of what young man is it recorded that "Jesus beholding him loved him"? ____________________
11. Where is the phrase used, "The chiefest among ten thousand"?
12. Who asked the question, "If a man die, shall he live again?"__

____
13. Who were the Seventy? ____________________

____
14. What is Isaiah's prescription for "perfect peace"? __________
15. What parable did Christ speak in answer to the question, "Who is my neighbor"? ____________________

16. What prophet, when Jerusalem was besieged by the Babylonians, showed his faith by buying a field in the country nearby in possession of the enemy? ________________

17. What was the feast of the dedication? ________________

18. What was Christ's claim to unity with God? ________________

____

19. What prophet saw the vision of the valley of dry bones? ________________

20. With whom was Christ talking when he urged him to get "treasure in heaven," and how was he to get it? ________________

____

21. What was the other name of Thomas? ________________

____

22. In what Book is the prophecy fulfilled by Christ's triumphal entry into Jerusalem? ________________

23. Who was Elymas, where did he live, and what was his other name? ________________

24. Of what family is it said that Jesus loved them? ________________

____

25. To whom did Christ say, "But one thing is needful," and of whom was he speaking? ________________

26. When did Saul, apparently, begin to be called by his Latin name, Paul? ________________

27. What is the origin of our phrase, "the powers that be"? ________________

28. In which Epistle is Paul's account of the institution of the Lord's Supper, so often used in our communion services? ________________

____

29. Locate the phrases, "Fair as the moon, clear as the sun, and terrible as an army with banners." ________________

30. What friend alone was with Paul in his last imprisonment? ________________

____

31. Where did Mary and Martha live, and where was the village?
32. To what country did Jacob go to find a wife, and where was it?
33. In what Epistle is Paul's list of the "whole armor of God"?
34. What words were engraved on the front of the high priest's mitre?
35. Where is the phrase, "Ye prisoners of hope"?
36. What is Paul's "Epistle of Joy"?
37. Where did Jacob have his vision of a "ladder" reaching to heaven, and what does the name mean?
38. Who was Alexander the coppersmith?
39. What famous Nazirite was among the Judges?
40. Whom had the writer of Hebrews in mind when he wrote, "Of whom the world was not worthy"?
41. Whom did Ruth marry?
42. Who was the first king of the Northern Kingdom, Israel?
43. Who was it called the wife "the weaker vessel"?
44. Who was David's first wife?
45. What is meant by Armageddon?
46. What two places of worship did Jeroboam establish in the Northern Kingdom, to take the place of Jerusalem?
47. Who killed Jezebel?
48. Where is the reference to Christ's preaching to "the spirits in prison"?
49. Who was Manoah?
50. What is the most famous vow of the tithe in the Bible?

SERIES XXVII

1. In what connection did Christ say that a camel could go through the eye of a needle easier than a rich man enter the kingdom of God? ________________
2. What persons of the name of Lazarus are mentioned in the Bible? ________________
3. Who was Sergius Paulus? ________________
4. Complete the quotation: "Love is strong as death;__________."
5. Whom did Christ send forth "as lambs among wolves"? ________________
6. Where are the famous verses beginning, "Intreat me not to leave thee__________thy people shall be my people," etc.? ______
7. Who was Asa? ________________
8. What parable did Christ end with the words, "Go, and do thou likewise"? ________________
9. Who was Ezra? ________________
10. Where is the sentence, "I am escaped with the skin of my teeth"? ________________
11. Who wrote the last Book of the Old Testament, and what does his name mean? ________________
12. What is the rest of the prayer sentence, "Lead me to the rock ________________"?
13. What Old Testament happening did Christ use to illustrate his coming three days in the grave? ________________
14. Who was Zerah? ________________
15. Finish the quotation from Malachi: "Then they that feared the Lord ________________."

16. What Old Testament happening did Christ use to rebuke the heedlessness of his generation to his teachings? ____________
17. What reform did Ezra bring about when he went to Jerusalem? ____________
18. Finish the proverb: "A good name is rather to be chosen____."
19. In what connection did Christ say that he came "not to be ministered unto, but to minister"? ____________
20. What great mistake was made by Asa? ____________
21. Where is the wonderful sentence, "I know that my redeemer liveth," etc.? ____________
22. What miracle did Christ work in Jericho? ____________
23. In what connection were the words used, "The Lord hath need of him"? ____________
24. What was Christ's only miracle of destruction? ____________
25. On what occasion did Christ speak of the clean "outside of the cup," the inside being foul? ____________
26. In connection with what parable did Christ say, "Ask, and it shall be given you," etc.? ____________
27. Who anointed Christ's feet with costly spikenard? ____________
28. What happened to King Jeroboam when he put out his hand to seize one of God's prophets? ____________
29. What is the first part of the proverb ending "and when he is old, he will not depart from it"? ____________
30. What is the most notable occasion on which the shout, "Hosanna!" was heard? ____________
31. Who was the prophet Hanani? ____________
32. With what prophecy looking forward to the New Testament does the Old Testament close? ____________
33. Of whom is it said, "They loved the praise of men more than the praise of God"? ____________

34. What king of Israel was slain as he was "drinking himself drunk"? ____________
35. On what occasion did Christ wash his disciples' feet, and why? ____________
36. Who founded the city of Samaria to be the northern capital? ____________
37. What king of Israel reigned only seven days? ____________
38. On what occasion did Christ say, "I am the way, the truth, and the life"? ____________
39. How long did Jacob serve for Rachel? ____________
40. When did Christ promise to send the Holy Spirit to his followers? ____________
41. What is "the Mizpah benediction" and on what occasion was it first spoken? ____________
42. Where was the first missionary sermon of which we have an extended report preached? ____________
43. Who made the golden calf and who destroyed it? ____________
44. Where did Paul first turn definitely to the Gentiles in his missionary work? ____________
45. Whom did Jacob marry before he was allowed to marry Rachel? ____________
46. When was Moses compelled to cover his face with a veil? ____________
47. Where did Paul use the famous comparison of the members of Christ's church to the members of the body? ____________
48. At what place did the angels meet Jacob as he left Laban? ____________
49. What is the great Love Chapter of the Bible? ____________
50. What is the great Resurrection Chapter of the Bible? ____________

SERIES XXVIII

1. Locate: "Many waters cannot quench love." ________________
2. In what connection did Christ say, "With God all things are possible"? ________________
3. What was Christ's greatest miracle, with the exception of his resurrection? ________________
4. When did Christ see Satan as lightning falling from heaven? ________________
5. In what Book is the chief Bible passage regarding tithes? ________________
6. From what village was the colt taken on which Christ made his triumphal entry into Jerusalem? ________________
7. What happened to Jacob at Peniel, by the ford of the Jabbok? ________________
8. Who was Deborah (*not* the prophetess)? ________________
9. Who was the strongest man of the Bible? ________________
10. Who received as a sign of favor a coat of many colors? ________________
11. How did Michal save David from Saul? ________________
12. Who was Rachel's first son? and her second? ________________
13. Who were king and queen of Israel when Elijah began his work? ________________
14. Where did Elijah live? ________________
15. What is the only miracle related in all four Gospels? ________________
16. What Old Testament character was noted for his dreams and interpretation of the dreams of others? ________________

17. To whom and on what occasion did Christ say, "O thou of little faith, wherefore didst thou doubt?" ______________________

____

18. What Bible character made riddles? ______________________
19. Whom did Christ call "blind leaders of the blind"? __________
20. Who found a piece of money in a fish? ____________________

____

21. Who gave a signal to David by shooting arrows? ____________
22. In what Zidonian city did Elijah find refuge? ______________
23. At what place was Joseph sold by his brothers? ____________
24. Who received the keys of the kingdom of heaven? __________
25. Where did Joash spend the first six years of his life? _________

____

26. On what occasion was a present given in three instalments?___

____

27. In obeying Christ, how many times should we forgive a wrong-doer? ____
28. What is the origin of our phrase, "eleventh hour repentance"?

____

____

29. Which of Christ's parables contains the request, "Give us of your oil"? ______________________________________
30. What part was played by the cave of Adullam? _____________

____

31. Of what was Christ speaking when he referred to "the sheep and the goats"? __________________________________
32. Which two of Joseph's brothers sought to save his life from the other brothers? ______________________________
33. What two things did Elijah do for the widow of Zarephath?___

____

34. Who slew a thousand men with the jawbone of an ass? ________
35. What high priest presided over the Sanhedrin which condemned Jesus? ________
36. Who was Necho? ________
37. How did David twice prove to Saul that Saul's life had been in his hands and had been spared? ________

____
38. For how much did Judas betray Christ? ________

____
39. What queen began her reign by destroying all but one of the royal family? ________
40. What is the greatest occasion on which a hymn was ever sung?

____
41. What is the meaning of the reference, "a Judas kiss"? ________

____
42. In what city was Paul stoned? ________
43. Who gave Jacob his second name, Israel? ________

____
44. Who was Malchus? ________

____
45. Who was Joseph's master in Egypt? ________
46. Who presided over the first church council and rendered a decision? ________
47. Who was Jehoiada? ________

____
48. On Paul's second missionary journey who took the place of Barnabas, and who of Mark? ________
49. How many times did Peter deny Christ, and how many times did the cock crow? ________
50. Who was Abigail? ________

SERIES XXIX

1. What was Christ's greatest claim to power? ________________
2. Who was Ebed-melech? ________________
3. Why is Palm Sunday so called? ________________

____
4. Who was Jehosheba? ________________
5. Which of Joseph's fellow prisoners was restored to office and which was executed, as Joseph foretold? ________________

____
6. What woman cut off Samson's long hair and so destroyed his strength? ________________
7. What famous teaching did Christ draw from a Roman penny (denarius)? ________________
8. Among what heathen tribe did David take refuge in fleeing from Saul? ________________
9. Who was Asenath? ________________
10. What mistake do we make when we talk about "the widow's mite"? ________________
11. What is the origin of the common phrase, "tarrying by the stuff"? ________________

____
12. In what connection did Christ say, "She hath done what she could"? ________________
13. What witch did Saul consult before his last battle? ________________
14. Who were Joseph's two sons? ________________
15. In what garden did Christ suffer just before his arrest, and what does its name mean? ________________

16. Why did the Sanhedrin deliver Christ to Pilate? ____________
____
17. What were Christ's "seven words from the cross"? ___________
____
18. Whom did the Jews ask to be released rather than Jesus? _____
____
19. In what city did blind Samson overthrow the house and destroy his enemies? ______________________________
20. Which of Joseph's brothers offered to become a slave in order to save Benjamin? ______________________________
21. Who helped Christ bear his cross? _______________________
22. For what were the Christians of Berea noted? ______________
23. Who was Ish-bosheth? ___________________________________
24. What two names of the hill on which Christ was crucified, and what do they mean? _______________________________
25. What was the starting point of Paul's address at Athens?_____
____
26. Who said, "Thy love to me was wonderful, passing the love of women," and of whom was he speaking? _________________
27. In what part of Egypt did Jacob and his sons settle? _________
28. Locate the sentence, "Go ye into all the world, and preach the gospel to every creature." ____________________________
29. Who said, "There is a prince and a great man fallen this day in Israel," and of whom did he say it? ______________________
30. Where is the famous prophecy to be found foretelling the eminence of the tribe of Judah "until Shiloh come"? _____________
31. Where did Paul see "the Macedonian vision"? ______________
32. In what names did Christ command his followers to baptize?
____
33. Why were Paul and Silas imprisoned at Philippi? ___________

34. In what city was it said, in reference to Paul and his fellow missionaries, "These that have turned the world upside down are come hither also"? ____________________

35. Locate the sentence, "His bow abode in strength." ____________________

36. Where did Paul speak in Athens? ____________________

37. Why was Uzzah smitten? ____________________

38. With whom did Paul lodge at Corinth, and why with them? ____________________

39. What Roman ruler in Corinth refused to hear a charge against Paul? ____________________

40. Who was Apollos? ____________________

41. Who furnished a new tomb for the body of Jesus? ____________________

42. Where did Paul teach during two years at Ephesus? ____________________

43. What young man disastrously fell asleep under Paul's preaching? ____________________

44. In what Book is the true picture of a drunkard, beginning, "Who hath woe?" ____________________

45. Where did Paul, on his journey to Jerusalem, have an affecting interview with the elders of the church in Ephesus? ____________________

46. Who hid a hundred prophets in a cave and fed them with bread and water? ____________________

47. What put an end to Paul's work in Ephesus? ____________________

48. Where did Elijah conduct his great contest with the Baal priests? ____________________

49. How did the converts at Ephesus prove their sincerity? ____________________

50. What great purpose did David form and what prophet forbade its execution? ____________________

SERIES XXX

1. Finish Paul's sentence, "When I am weak__________________."
2. What prophet spoke of "the Sun of righteousness" arising "with healing in his wings"? __________________________
3. Complete these pairs: Adam and_________; Cain and_________; David and_________; Mary and__________; John and__________; Paul and__________; Ananias and________; Ruth and__________; Elijah and__________; Aquila and_________.
4. Who was Mephibosheth? ____________________________
5. What is a saying of Christ's that is not recorded in the Gospels, and who has given it to us? ___________________________
6. Locate the question, "How long halt ye between two opinions?" ____
7. What Christian leader had four daughters who were prophets?
8. Who was Uriah the Hittite? ___________________________
9. Who was the orator from Jerusalem who brought charges against Paul before Felix? ____________________________
10. Who was Trophimus? _________________________________
11. What is the origin of the sentence, "Eat, drink, and be merry"?
____
12. What was the name of the high priest whom Paul called a "whited wall"? ___________________________________
13. Who was Jedidiah? __________________________________
14. What was the name of the chief captain who arrested Paul in Jerusalem? ___________________________________
15. Where in the Bible is the reference to "a little cloud, like a man's hand"? ____________________________________

16. Who was the Roman governor of Palestine before whom Paul was first tried? and the second governor? ____________________

17. Who was the wise woman of Tekoah? ____________________
18. What Roman governor promised to hear Paul when he had "a convenient season"? ____________________
19. In connection with what event is a juniper tree mentioned?____
20. Whom did Christ call "that fox"? ____________________
21. What favorite son of David rebelled against him?__________
22. Before whom was Paul speaking when he said, "I was not disobedient unto the heavenly vision"? ____________________
23. What is the origin of the expression, "highways and hedges"?
24. What is the best loved of the parables, and in which Gospel is it found? ____________________
25. Who was Ahithophel? ____________________
26. What Book of the Bible is about the return of a runaway slave? What was the slave's name, and the name of his master? ____________________
27. In what parable is the phrase, "a great gulf fixed"?__________

28. Who was Shimei? ____________________
29. Which parable contains the words, "God be merciful to me a sinner"? ____________________
30. What rich man climbed into a sycomore tree to see Jesus?____
31. How did Absalom die? ____________________
32. Who was Bernice? ____________________
33. What two enemies became friends during the trial of Jesus?__

34. What three languages were used in the inscriptions on Christ's cross? ____________________

35. To what does "the chamber over the gate" refer? ____________
____
36. Where in the Bible is the reference to "a still small voice"?____
____
37. Who was Julius? ______________________________________
38. Where were two disciples going on the afternoon of the first Easter when the risen Lord joined them? And what was the name of one of them? __________________________________
39. What gift did David dedicate to God, refusing it for himself as too precious? ____
40. Complete Isaiah's eloquent sentence beginning, "How beautiful upon the mountains____________." ____________________
41. Of what do we think when we read, "He cast his mantle upon him"? ____
42. What king of Judah, fighting as an ally of Ahab king of Israel, nearly lost his life through being mistaken for Ahab?_________
43. Who was Naboth? _____________________________________
____
44. What verse of the Bible contains all the letters of the alphabet except J? ____
45. Locate the phrase, "Whose I am, and whom I serve."_________
____
46. What is the longest verse in the Bible?_____________________
47. On what island was Paul shipwrecked on the way to Rome?
____
48. How many Books in the Bible, how many chapters, how many verses, how many words, and how many letters? ____________
____
49. Who was Publius? ____________________________________
50. What is the middle verse of the Bible? ____________________

SERIES I.

1. Bethlehem.
2. Nathan to David; 2 Sam. 12:7.
3. The Book of Nehemiah.
4. The passover; Ex. 12:22. The crucifixion of Jesus; John 19:29.
5. "Come ye to the waters"; Isa. 55:1.
6. James and Jude.
7. "All things whatsoever ye would that men should do to you, do ye even so to them"; Matt. 7:12.
8. Philippi; Acts 16:12. 13.
9. John the Baptist, John the apostle, and John Mark, usually called Mark.
10. Job; see Job 1:9.
11. Jephthah; Judg. 11:31-40.
12. Jonah; see Jonah 4:1-11.
13. Christ's parable of "the pearl of great price"; Matt. 13:45, 46.
14. Rachel; Gen. 29:18-20.
15. To take care of the temple; Num. 8:23-26.
16. Mt. Hermon, 9,166 above the sea.
17. "A glad father"; Prov. 10:1.
18. Jeremiah; see Jer. 38:10-13.
19. In the New Jerusalem; Rev. 22:2.
20. David in the Twenty-third Psalm.
21. In Jude, the last two verses.
22. James 3:1-18.
23. Job 37:1-14.
24. "Every idle word that men shall speak, they shall give account thereof in the day of judgment"; Matt. 12:36.
25. In the wilderness near Mt. Horeb; Ex. 3:1, 2.
26. Andrew; John 1:40.
27. Lydia; Acts 16:14, 15.
28. Ps. 90: "Lord, thou hast been our dwelling place in all generations."
29. The first cousin and foster father of Esther; see Esth. 2:7.
30. When they mocked Elisha; 2 Kings 2:24.
31. It was made by Moses and placed on a pole for the people to look at and be healed of the bites of a plague of serpents; Num. 21:5-9.
32. 1 Cor. 13.
33. Ps. 119 (176 verses).
34. "Even Christ pleased not himself"; Rom. 15:3.
35. The Jordan.
36. Five thousand (Matt. 14:21). Four thousand (Matt. 15:38).
37. Levi; compare Matt. 9:9 with Mark 2:14.
38. Jonathan; 1 Sam. 18:1.
39. The Ten Commandments; Ex. 20:1-17.
40. "Let us kneel before the Lord our maker"; Ps. 95:6.
41. "The evidence of things not seen"; Heb. 11:1.
42. A man bearing a pitcher of water; Mark 14:12-16.
43. Locusts and wild honey; Mark 1:6.
44. Sea of Chinnereth (Num. 34:11); Lake of Gennesaret (Luke 5:1); Sea of Tiberias (John 6:1).
45. "And so fulfil the law of Christ"; Gal. 6:2.
46. Ezekiel; see Ezek. 47:1-5.
47. To a quiver full of arrows; Ps. 127:4, 5.
48. Joash; 2 Kings 11:1-3.
49. Jochebed; Num. 26:59.
50. The fig-tree, Gen. 3:7; for it is not said what kind of tree was "the tree of the knowledge of good and evil," Gen. 2:17,—traditionally held to have been an apple-tree.

SERIES II.

1. The father of Samuel; 1 Sam. 1:1, 2, 19, 20.
2. Amoz was the father of Isaiah, Isa. 1:1; Amos was one of the Minor Prophets.
3. "The way of the ungodly shall perish"; Ps. 1:6.
4. Abraham, David, and Solomon; Matt. 1:1-16.
5. "Hexateuch" (meaning "six books") is the first six Books of the Bible: Genesis, Exodus, Leviticus, Numbers, Deuteronomy, and Joshua.
6. "Old Hundred"; Ps. 100.

SERIES II.—Continued.

7. Paul, in Rom. 1:16.
8. The brother of Nehemiah, who brought him news of the sad condition of Jerusalem; Neh. 1:1-3.
9. Exodus.
10. Uzziah, king of Judah; 2 Chron. 26:10.
11. 1 and 2 Thessalonians and Philippians.
12. On the first day, light; second, the firmament; third, earth, seas, and vegetation; fourth, heavenly bodies; fifth, fishes and birds; sixth, beasts and man. See Gen. 1:1-31.
13. Joseph; Matt. 1:18, 19.
14. Nadab and Abihu, sons of Aaron; Num. 3:4.
15. 1 Samuel, 2 Samuel, 1 Kings and 2 Kings.
16. With a camel's hair robe and a leather girdle; Mark 1:6.
17. Ahaziah; 2 Kings 1:2.
18. Reuben, Simeon, Judah, Issachar, Zebulun, Benjamin, Dan, Naphtali, Gad, Asher, Ephraim, and Manasseh. Levi was scattered among the other tribes, and the last two were the tribes of the sons of Joseph. See Gen. 48:5; Ex. 1:1-5.
19. In the land of Moab; Deut. 1:5.
20. John, who lived to be nearly a hundred.
21. Judges.
22. "Jehovah is salvation"; Matt. 1:21.
23. The Revelation (not "Revelations") of St. John the Divine.
24. Joshua; see Josh. 1:1-5.
25. "Grace and truth came by Jesus Christ"; John 1:17.
26. Adam, signifying "Man"; Gen. 5:2.
27. Joshua; see Josh 1:6.
28. The Philistines; 1 Sam. 5:1.
29. Joshua.
30. Baal-zebub (Beelzebub); 2 Kings 1:3.
31. Mark; see Acts 13:5 (Mark's full name being John Mark). Also Luke, written by Paul's physician; Col. 4:14.
32. To Moses at Mt. Horeb; Deut. 1:5, 6.
33. Athaliah; 2 Kings 11:1.
34. The king was the Pharaoh of Egypt; Ex. 1:8.
35. Of Christ; John 1:4.
36. Manasseh.
37. The high priest Jehoiada; 2 Kings 12:9.
38. In Bethlehem; Matt. 2:1.
39. Corinth.
40. "Be glorified"; 2 Thess. 3:1.
41. The saying of John the Baptist that he was not worthy to unloose the "latchet" of Christ's shoes; Mark 1:7.
42. Jerusalem; Isa. 1:1.
43. The two Books of Chronicles.
44. Esther; Hadassah; see Esth. 2:7.
45. David, Ps. 22:1; quoted by Christ on the cross, Mark 15:34.
46. In the interior of Asia Minor; Gal. 1:2.
47. Judah, because the nearest portion of Canaan had been assigned to that tribe; Judges 1:1-4.
48. Hezekiah, king of Judah; 2 Kings 20:1-11.
49. The Levites; Num. 2:17.
50. Hebrews (the reference to Paul in the title is much later than the original manuscript; some scholars think Hebrews was written by Apollos.)

SERIES III.

1. I Thessalonians.
2. Nehemiah, cupbearer to Artaxerxes; Neh. 1:11.
3. Paul; 1 Thess. 5:17.
4. Acts; Theophilus; compare Luke 1:3 with Acts 1:1.
5. "Pentateuch" (meaning five books) is the first five Books of the Bible: Genesis, Exodus, Leviticus, Numbers, and Deuteronomy.
6. Ruth; see Matt. 1:5.
7. Uzziah; 2 Chron. 26:16-21.
8. "There is no God" (Ps. 14:1).
9. Genesis (2:1-3).

SERIES III.—Continued.

10. Zacharias was the father of John the Baptist, Luke 1:5; Zechariah was the prophet who wrote the next to the last Book of the Old Testament.
11. Forty; see Deut. 1:3.
12. Saul, after the battle of Gilboa; 1 Chron. 10:1-4.
13. Enoch; Gen. 5:24.
14. Corinth; 1 Cor. 1:12.
15. Jeremiah; he wrote the Lamentations; see also Jer. 9:1, etc.
16. Xerxes; Esth. 1:1.
17. God.
18. In connection with the Hebrew captivity in Egypt; Ex. 1:11.
19. Joel.
20. For the seven churches of Asia; Rev. 1:4.
21. Bashan was a country east of the Jordan.
22. Immediately after his conversion; Gal. 1:15-18.
23. The firstborn son, because the Hebrew firstborn sons were preserved when all those in Egypt were destroyed; Num. 3:13.
24. James; see Jas. 1:4.
25. Daniel.
26. Ps. 22:18; with the parting of Christ's garments among the soldiers at his crucifixion.
27. The Euphrates; Deut. 1:7, and elsewhere.
28. "The fear of the Lord"; Ps. 111:10.
29. One of the minor prophets, teaching in Judah.
30. Solomon; Prov. 5:15.
31. By a whirlwind; 2 Kings 2:1, 11.
32. Josh. 1:8: "This book of the law shall not depart out of thy mouth; but thou shalt meditate therein day and night," etc.
33. "As far as the east is from the west, so far hath he removed our transgressions from us"; Ps. 103:12.
34. Lamech; Gen. 5:28, 29.
35. "Israel doth not know, my people doth not consider"; Isa. 1:3.
36. John the Baptist; Mark 1:8.
37. Because he had thus treated seventy other chieftains; Judg. 1:5-7.
38. The fair Shunammite maiden who cherished David in his old age; 1 Kings 1:1-4.
39. This is said of Christ in Heb. 1:3.
40. Levi; Ex. 2:1.
41. The national god of the Philistines, whose idol fell down before the ark; 1 Sam. 5:2-4.
42. The mother of John the Baptist; Luke 1:5.
43. Herod the Great; Matt. 2:1.
44. Hannah was the mother of Samuel; 1 Sam. 1:20; Anna was a prophetess in the temple who recognized the infant Christ as the Messiah; Luke 2:36-38.
45. Elijah: 2 Kings 1:9-15.
46. David's son, who made insurrection against him; 1 Kings 1:5.
47. The daughter of Caleb, to whom he gave water springs; Judg. 1:12-15.
48. Christ, just before his ascension; Acts 1:7.
49. Paul; Rom. 1:17.
50. Killed himself with his own sword; 1 Chron. 10:5.

SERIES IV.

1. Thessalonica.
2. Sanballat and Tobiah; Neh. 4:1-3.
3. Methuselah; 969 years; Gen. 5:27.
4. "In pleasant places"; Ps. 16:6.
5. Genesis.
6. Ps. 22:12.
7. Elkanah's wife, the rival of Hannah; I Sam. 1:2.
8. Obadiah, Philemon, 2 John, 3 John, and Jude.
9. Eden was probably around the head of the Persian Gulf.
10. "Seest thou a man diligent in his business? he shall stand before kings"; Prov. 22:29.
11. John the Baptist; John 1:23.

SERIES IV.—Continued.

12. Joash of Israel; 2 Kings 13:14-19.
13. Isa. 52:13—53:12.
14. Elisha; 2 Kings 2:1-6.
15. In Ezekiel (1:16).
16. Moses; Ex. 2:3.
17. Jesus, by John the Baptist; John 1:29.
18. Olivet; Acts 1:12.
19. They began at the age of twenty (probably for the lesser duties) to thirty (for the complete service), and ended at the age of fifty (Num. 4:3; 8:24; 1 Chron. 23:24, 27).
20. "Thou condemnest thyself"; Rom. 2:1.
21. Saul's; 1 Chron. 1:10.
22. Leviticus.
23. The wilderness between Sinai and Canaan; Deut. 1:19.
24. Hananiah, Mishael, and Azariah; Dan. 1:6.
25. On the southern frontier of Canaan.
26. He committed her to the care of John; John 19:25-27.
27. Capernaum ("village of Nahum").
28. It was the capital of King Xerxes (Ahasuerus) in southeastern Persia.
29. To Joshua; Josh. 1:9.
30. Paul's young and beloved helper.
31. Ecclesiastes.
32. Ps. 23.
33. Paul; 1 Cor. 1:21.
34. Jericho; Deut. 34:3.
35. Joel (2:13).
36. Jonas; Matt. 12:39, etc.
37. In Proverbs (6:6-8).
38. The angels; Heb. 1:14.
39. Luz; Judg. 1:23.
40. Wise men from the east who came to the infant Jesus; Matt. 2:1.
41. "Learn to do well"; Isaiah (1:16, 17).
42. Titus; Gal. 2:1-3.
43. The Lamentations of Jeremiah.
44. The ark of the covenant; 1 Sam. 6. 12.
45. That of a dove; Mark 1:10.
46. Bath-sheba; 1 Kings 1:11.
47. John the Baptist; Luke 1:15.
48. Nathan; 1 Kings 1:10-14.
49. Jesus Christ; Rev. 1:5.
50. It was the birthplace of Jeremiah; Jer. 1:1.

SERIES V.

1. "The glory of God," "his handy-work"; Ps. 19:1.
2. Ephesus, Smyrna, Pergamos, Thyatira, Sardis, Philadelphia, Laodicea.
3. Ezekiel; see Ezek. 1:1. Daniel; see Dan. 1:1-6.
4. The creation of the first woman; Gen. 2:20-24.
5. Jehovah.
6. Three.
7. Christ, to His apostles; Acts 1:8.
8. The Levites; Num. 3:44, 45.
9. Evil sons of Eli; 1 Sam. 2:12-17.
10. Enoch; Gen. 5:4.
11. 2 John.
12. One of the Egyptian treasure cities built by the Hebrew captives; Ex.. 1:11.
13. Some animal or bird entirely consumed upon the altar.
14. Hebron.
15. The star of Bethlehem; Matt. 2:1, 2.
16. They made them live outside the camp; later, outside the towns or cities; Num. 5:1-4.
17. Three times: at his baptism, Mark 1:11; at his transfiguration, Luke 9:35; and when the Greeks sought him in the temple, John 12:28.
18. Queen of Xerxes, whom he deposed; Esth. 1:9-12.
19. John the Baptist; Luke 1:17.
20. Caleb and Joshua, because they alone had faith to believe God's word that they could conquer Canaan; Deut. 1:35-38.
21. The archangel Gabriel; Luke 1:19, 26, etc. The Archangel Michael; Rev. 12:7, etc.
22. The room of the Lord's Supper (Mark 22:12) and of the assembling of the disciples after the ascension (Acts 1:13).

SERIES V.—Continued.

23. "The world, and they that dwell therein"; Ps. 24:1.
24. Because she sheltered the two spies whom Joshua sent into Jericho; Josh. 2:1-14.
25. Andrew and Philip; John 1:40, 41, 45. Doubtless also John, who brought his brother James.
26. "There is no respect of persons with God"; Rom. 2:11.
27. Some think it calls for a fresh outburst of voices or instruments; others that it calls for silence, like a rest in music.
28. Eglon, the king of Moab; Judg. 3:12-17.
29. "Wiser than men," "stronger than men"; 1 Cor. 1:25.
30. Hebron is about nineteen miles southwest of Jerusalem.
31. Simon Peter; Simon (Simeon) was his original name, to which Christ added Cephas, "a stone," an Aramaic word of which "Peter" is a translation into Greek.
32. Ecclesiastes; see 1:2; 12:8.
33. Because they looked into the ark of the covenant; 1 Sam. 6:19.
34. "A double minded man is unstable in all his ways"; Jas. 1:8.
35. They were unchanging and unchangeable; Esth. 1:19.
36. Signifying the completeness of his divine character, these being the first and last letters of the Greek alphabet; Rev. 1:8.
37. They were the hornlike extensions of the altar of burnt offerings in the tabernacle and temple, and criminals and others pursued were to be safe while they clung to them; 1 Kings 1:51.
38. Paul; Gal. 2:20.
39. Prov. 6:9-11: "How long wilt thou sleep, O sluggard?" etc.
40. "Christ Jesus came into the world to save sinners; of whom I am chief." So wrote Paul to Timothy, 1 Tim. 1:15.
41. One hundred and twenty; Acts 1:15.
42. The first of the Judges, who delivered the Israelites from the Mesopotamians; Judg. 3:8-10.
43. Matthias; Acts 1:26.
44. "As white as snow," "as wool"; Isa. 1:18.
45. Ezekiel; see Ezek. 2:1, 3, 6, 8, etc.
46. "So great salvation?" Heb. 2:3.
47. Members of the "schools of the prophets," theological schools, founded perhaps by Samuel; 2 Kings 2:3, 5.
48. Pulse (peas and beans) and water; Dan. 1:12.
49. "For in due season we shall reap, if we faint not"; Gal. 6:9.
50. Jeremiah (2:13).

SERIES VI.

1. Joseph (Ex. 37:3) and Samuel (1 Sam. 2:19).
2. The western portion of the continent, called by us Asia Minor.
3. Isaiah, Jeremiah, Ezekiel, and Daniel.
4. Nehemiah (4:6).
5. Kadesh-barnea; Num. 13:26.
6. From its two censuses, or numberings of the people; Num. 1:2; 26:2.
7. Genesis (2:24).
8. Hezekiah; 2 Kings 19:14-20.
9. In the last two chapters of Revelation.
10. "Be acceptable in thy sight, O Lord, my strength, and my redeemer" (Ps. 19:14).
11. Olivet.
12. John 11:35: "Jesus wept."
13. Of the time before the flood; Gen. 6:4.
14. Gold, frankincense, and myrrh (Matt. 2:11).
15. Male and female deities of the heathen tribes of Canaan; Judg. 2:13.
16. The forty days of temptation in the wilderness and the forty days between his resurrection and ascension.

SERIES VI.—Continued.

17. Miriam (Mary); Ex. 15:20.
18. "Remember the Sabbath day, to keep it holy"; Ex. 20:8-11.
19. The two spies at Jericho, Josh. 2:15; and Saul at Damascus, Acts 9:25.
20. Andrew and Peter, James and John, were fishers; Matthew was a tax-collector.
21. Capernaum.
22. Shem, Ham, and Japheth; Gen. 6:10.
23. Isaiah (2:4).
24. James and John; Mark 1:19.
25. "The Lord bless thee, and keep thee: the Lord make his face shine upon thee, and be gracious unto thee: the Lord lift up his countenance upon thee, and give thee peace"; Num. 6:24-27.
26. A vegetable offering, usually a cake of meal or unleavened bread; Lev. 2:1-16.
27. Because Christ healed his mother-in-law of a fever; Mark 1:30, 31.
28. "Precious in the sight of the Lord is the death of his saints"; Ps. 116:15.
29. The Capernaum leper; Mark 1:40.
30. When a babe, Christ was taken there by his parents to escape from Herod; Matt. 2:13-15.
31. Taking the cubit of 18 inches, the ark was 450 feet long, 75 feet wide, and 45 feet high; Gen. 6:15.
32. "The fear of the Lord"; Prov. 9:10.
33. The Virgin Mary; Luke 1:38.
34. He speaks of such men as "saying, Peace, peace; when there is no peace"; Jer. 6:14.
35. The king of Bashan, who opposed the passage of the Israelites; he was a giant and slept on an iron bedstead 13½ feet long; Deut. 3:1-11.
36. Ecclesiastes (1:9).
37. The hymn of Zacharias concerning his son, John the Baptist, beginning "Benedictus" in the Latin version (Luke 1:68-79).
38. Joab; 1 Kings 2:28-34.
39. "He hath put down the mighty from their seats"; Luke 1:52.
40. Joel (2:28).
41. When Elijah smote the Jordan with it, a passage was opened up through the water; 2 Kings 2:28.
42. Jesus, in the hymn of Zacharias; Luke 1:78, 79.
43. Nathanael; John 1:46.
44. Ezekiel (3:1-3).
45. David; 1 Chron. 2:5-7.
46. The Virgin Mary's hymn on visiting Elisabeth, beginning with *Magnificat* ("Magnifies") in the Latin version (Luke 1:46-55).
47. Nebuchadnezzar; Dan. 2:4, 5.
48. The coming of the Messiah and his crucifixion; Zech. 13:1.
49. To Tarshish (southern Spain), and from Joppa; Jonah 1:3.
50. A wicked officer of King Xerxes, who plotted against the Jews; Esth. 3:6.

SERIES VII.

1. Deuteronomy.
2. Hosea, Joel, Amos, Obadiah, Jonah, Micah, Nahum, Habakkuk, Zephaniah, Haggai, Zechariah, Malachi.
3. Ps. 20:1-4.
4. Two thousand cubits or about three thousand feet, a little more than half a mile.
5. Eve; Gen. 3:20.
6. Abraham, Caleb, and David; the last named made it his first capital.
7. Psalms—150.
8. The boy Samuel; 1 Sam. 3:8-10.
9. Xerxes (Ahasuerus); Esth. 1:22.
10. Bringing to Christ his brother, Simon Peter; John 1:40, 41
11. Nehemiah (6:3).
12. His wife and his three sons and their wives, and one each of every living creature, a male and a female; Gen. 6:18-20.
13. Nathanael; John 1:47.
14. Paul; "The law was our schoolmaster to bring us unto Christ"; Gal. 3:24.

SERIES VII.—Continued.

15. Because it was celebrated fifty days after the beginning of barley harvest and marked the close of the grain harvest.
16. "Bodily exercises profiteth little"; 1 Tim. 4:8.
17. The turning of water into wine, at Cana of Galilee; John 2:1-11.
18. "Thou shalt not kill"; Ex. 20:13.
19. The early Christians; Acts 2:44.
20. No such Book as Ahaziah; 3 John has only one chapter; we have only two Epistles of Peter.
21. Twice, at the beginning and the end of his ministry; John 2:13-17; Luke 19:45, 46.
22. "And sharper than any twoedged sword"; Heb. 4:12.
23. Two; it is Psalm 117.
24. He was a prisoner on the isle of Patmos off the coast of Asia Minor.
25. Probably the miraculous ability to speak in languages before unknown to the speakers; Acts 2:4-8.
26. Forty days; Gen. 7:12.
27. The glorified Christ seen by John in his Revelation (1:16).
28. Objects placed in the high priest's breastplate and drawn therefrom for purposes of divination; Lev. 8:8.
29. To the land of Midian, in Arabia, northeast of the Red Sea.
30. Ehud; Judg. 3:15-30.
31. The early church in Jerusalem; Acts 2:47.
32. Wisdom; 1 Kings 3:5-15.
33. Jacob, Gen. 29:10; and Moses, Ex. 2:17.
34. A cairn of twelve stones from the bed of the river, set up at Gilgal; Josh 5:20.
35. The church of Corinth; 1 Cor. 2:2.
36. By pretending to intend to divide the child between them with a sword, when the real mother begged him to give the child to the other woman rather than slay it; 1 Kings 3:16-28.
37. Shamgar; Judg. 3:31.
38. The death angel's passing over the houses of the Israelites in Egypt as he went on to kill the firstborn of the Egyptians.
39. Elisha; 2 Kings 2:15.
40. "For they shall inherit the earth"; Matt. 5:5.
41. The draught from the well of Bethlehem, which three of his warriors risked their lives to obtain; 1 Chron. 11:15-19.
42. Esther, to spur her to try to save her people; Esth. 4:14.
43. "The things which God hath prepared for them that love him"; 1 Cor. 2:9.
44. "My heart said unto thee, Thy face, Lord, will I seek"; Ps. 27:8.
45. The ark was kept there after its return from the Philistines; 1 Sam. 7:1.
46. On Mt. Ararat, in Armenia; Gen. 8:4.
47. "Abomination to the Lord," "his delight"; Prov. 11:1.
48. It was the mountain northeast of the Dead Sea from which Moses got a view of the land of Canaan which he was not permitted to enter; Deut. 3:25-27.
49. "Light excelleth darkness"; Eccl. 2:13.
50. Elijah; 2 Kings 2:12.

SERIES VIII.

1. The mother of Moses, Ex. 2:9.
2. The coming of the Holy Spirit to the early church; Acts 2:1.
3. "The beginning of knowledge"; Prov. 1:7.
4. The raven sent forth by Noah from the ark, Gen. 8:6, 7; the ravens which fed Elijah, 1 Kings 17:2-7.
5. With that of Rahab, who was preserved in the fall of Jericho by the token of a scarlet thread in her window; Josh. 2:18.

SERIES VIII.—Continued.

6. At the eastern entrance of the Garden of Eden; Gen. 3:24.
7. It was a meeting place of the Israelites in the time of Samuel; 1 Sam. 7:5, etc.
8. The sacrifice of an animal as an act of gratitude or devotion or in payment of a vow, followed by the eating of a part of the cooked flesh, the remainder going to the priests; Lev. 3:1-17.
9. Every one dwelling at home, a time of peace; 1 Kings 4:25.
10. The tabernacle was there from the time of Joshua, Josh 18:1, to that of Samuel, 1 Sam. 3:21.
11. Elisha; 2 Kings 2:19-22.
12. Nehemiah (6:11).
13. "Thou shalt not covet"; Ex. 20:17.
14. Reuel. Ex. 2:18; also called Jethro, Ex. 3:1.
15. Esther; Esth. 4:16.
16. "In the multitude of counsellors there is safety"; Prov. 11:14.
17. The Lord's mercies and compassions; Lam. 3:23.
18. The dove bearing an olive leaf; Gen. 8:11.
19. Moses; Deut. 4:29.
20. "Let us walk"; Isa. 2:5.
21. The battle of Mizpąh (Mizpeh); 1 Sam. 7:9-11.
22. "Then the Lord will take me up"; Ps. 27:10.
23. The wife of Moses; Ex. 2:21.
24. Solomon; see 1 Kings 4:29-31.
25. When the Israelites reached Canaan, and began to eat of the old corn of the land; Josh. 5:12.
26. Ecclesiastes (3:1).
27. Belteshazzar; Dan. 2:26.
28. Joshua; Josh. 5:13-15.
29. That he brings misfortune, as the sailors thought that Jonah had brought the great storm upon their ship; Jonah 1:4-12.
30. "For they shall see God"; Matt. 5:8.
31. Gershom and Eliezer; Ex. 18:3, 4.
32. "Knoweth them that trust in him"; Nahum 1:7.
33. "While the earth remaineth, seedtime and harvest, and cold and heat, and summer and winter, and day and night shall not cease"; Gen. 8:22.
34. "We are not saved"; Jer. 8:20.
35. A mighty general of the Canaanites, who held the Israelites in subjection for twenty years; Judg. 4:2, 3.
36. Ezekiel (Ezek. 4:4-8).
37. Brother of Moses and the first high priest of Israel.
38. Daniel (2:35, 45).
39. Eben-ezer means "stone of help," and was the name given to a stone set up by Samuel to commemorate the triumph which God gave his army in the battle of Mizpah; 1 Sam. 7:12.
40. He was let down through a hole they made in the roof; Mark 2:1-4.
41. Those forbidden to be eaten, such as swine, hares, eels, and owls; Lev. 11.
42. Jesus; John 2:25.
43. Herod's killing of all the children of Bethlehem and vicinity that were two years old or under; Matt 2:16.
44. The Beautiful Gate; Acts 3:2.
45. On the fourteenth of the month Abib (later called Nisan), the beginning of the Jewish year, corresponding roughly to our March; Num. 9:5. It lasts seven days; Ex. 12:15.
46. Cæsar Augustus; Luke 2:1.
47. They remained in one place as long as the pillar of cloud and fire rested on the tabernacle; Num. 9:22, 23.
48. Nazareth in Galilee.
49. "In the valley of decision"; Joel 3:14.
50. "We will rejoice and be glad in it"; Ps. 118:24.

SERIES IX.

1. Dan was a town at the northern extremity of Palestine and Beer-sheba at the southern extremity, so that the phrase means "throughout Palestine"; see 1 Sam. 3:20.
2. Sisera; Judg. 4:3.
3. Three thousand; 1 Kings 4:32.
4. "In the sight of any bird"; Prov. 1:17.
5. Jeremiah (31:15).
6. Cain; Gen. 4:1.
7. Archelaus; Matt. 2:22.
8. Samuel said it when he set up Ebenezer, "the stone of help"; 1 Sam. 7:12.
9. Ezra; Neh. 8:8.
10. "Every man a liar"; Rom. 3:4.
11. Exodus (20:1-17) and Deuteronomy (5:6-21).
12. Jericho; Josh. 6:20.
13. Deborah; Judg. 4:5.
14. That he "shall be made fat"; Prov. 11:25.
15. "I have planted, Apollos watered; but God gave the increase"; 1 Cor. 3:6.
16. "A threefold cord is not quickly broken"; Eccl. 4:12.
17. Balm (balsam), used to treat wounds; Jer. 8:22.
18. Saul, son of Kish; 1 Sam. 9:1, 2.
19. In Isaiah (3:16-24).
20. Obed-edom; 1 Chron. 13:14.
21. That it "leaveneth the whole lump"; Gal. 5:9.
22. The miracle of the ditches filled with water without rain; 2 Kings 3:6-27.
23. "Worship the Lord"; Ps. 29:2.
24. Hiram; 1 Kings 5:1.
25. Haman was hanged on the gallows which he had prepared for Mordecai; Esth. 7:10.
26. That it is "great gain"; 1 Tim. 6:6.
27. Daniel's three friends, Shadrach, Meshach, and Abednego, because they refused to worship Nebuchadnezzar's image; Dan. 3:1-23.
28. A very strict Jewish sect, bitter haters of the Romans, ardent patriots, and so the popular party.
29. "—— the yoke in his youth"; Lam. 3:27.
30. John the Baptist, in attacks on the sins of his times; Matt. 3:10.
31. That he "was in all points tempted like as we are, yet without sin"; Heb. 4:15.
32. "Thou shalt not make unto thee any graven image"; Ex. 20:4-6.
33. Those of the patch of new cloth on an old garment and the new wine in an old wineskin; Mark 2:16, 17.
34. When fault was found with him for associating with publicans and sinners; Mark 2:16, 17.
35. "Pure religion and undefiled before God and the Father is this, To visit the fatherless and widows in their affliction, and to keep himself unspotted from the world"; Jas. 1:27.
36. A Jewish sect opposed to the Pharisees, fewer in number, better educated, wealthier, freer in their beliefs, denying immortality and the resurrection, high in authority in the church.
37. The angel's words to the Bethlehem shepherds; Luke 2:10.
38. "For theirs is the kingdom of heaven"; Matt. 5:3.
39. That of Ephesus; Rev. 2:4.
40. At the threat of the fiery furnace; Dan. 3:5, 7, 10, 15.
41. To Noah and his sons after the Flood; Gen. 9:6.
42. To Mary Magdalene; John 20:1, 11-18.
43. John the Baptist's; Matt. 3:2.
44. At the burning bush; Ex. 3:5.
45. The palsied man at Capernaum; Mark 2:11.
46. The Bethlehem manger that became a cradle for the infant Jesus; Luke 2:7.
47. A goat over whose head the sins of the people were confessed, that he might bear them away into the wilderness; Lev. 16:10, 21.
48. Nicodemus; John 3:1, 2.
49. In Tekoa, five miles south of Bethlehem.
50. To Hobab, the son of his father-in-law; Num. 10:29.

SERIES X.

1. In Ramah, 1 Sam. 7:17.
2. To Nicodemus; John 3:3.
3. By the Philistines, when they heard that the ark had been brought into the camp of the Hebrews; 1 Sam. 4:6-9.
4. The Pharisees and Sadducees; Matt. 3:8.
5. "Glory to God in the highest, and on earth peace, good will toward men"; Luke 2:14.
6. Nehemiah; see Neh. 13:15-22.
7. It was a magnificent colonnade on the east side of the temple; Acts 3:11.
8. Cain; Gen. 4:8.
9. One thousand and five; 1 Kings 4:32.
10. "And lean not unto thine own understanding" (Prov. 3:5).
11. By merely bidding him stretch it out; Mark 3:5.
12. Peter, to the lame man at the Beautiful Gate of the temple; Acts 3:6.
13. "In due time Christ died for the ungodly"; Rom. 5:6.
14. That there should be no more flood; Gen. 9:13-15.
15. Absolute existence, "I am that I am"; Ex. 3:14.
16. "Together with God"; 1. Cor. 3:9.
17. Nimrod; Gen. 10:8, 9.
18. "And I will give thee a crown of life"; Rev. 2:10.
19. "A land flowing with milk and honey"; Ex. 3:17.
20. The Virgin Mary; Luke 2:19.
21. To the mysterious coming of the wind; John 3:8.
22. The tenth day of the seventh month (roughly, our October), the annual day of expiation of the sins of the people; Lev. 16:29, 30.
23. Shem and Japheth; thence came the curse of Canaan, the son of Ham; Gen. 9:20-27.
24. A place in the wilderness where the people murmured against God and were punished by fire from the Lord; Num. 11:1-3.
25. Seventy men, appointed to aid Moses in the government; Num. 11:16, 17.
26. Four: Ex. 13:2-10, 11-17; Deut. 6:4-9; 11:13-21. (Good passages to commit to memory.)
27. Barak; Judg. 4:6-9.
28. Simeon; Luke 2:25.
29. When Joshua complained because Eldad and Medad prophesied in the camp; Num. 11:24-29.
30. The people asked this when Saul suddenly began to prophesy after Samuel had told him that he was to be king; 1 Sam. 10:5-12.
31. Cedar and fir timbers from Lebanon in return for Solomon's wheat and oil; 1 Kings 5:7-11.
32. For the establishment of many languages which occurred there, the Lord thus rebuking human pride and preventing men from combining against him; Gen. 11:1-9.
33. To himself, lifted on the cross, that those who looked upon him in faith might live; John 3:14, 15.
34. He caused all the vessels she could obtain to be filled miraculously with oil, which she sold to pay her debts and to live on; 2 Kings 4:1-7.
35. With a victory won by David over the Philistines; 1 Chron. 14:13-17.
36. His rod thrown to the ground would become a serpent, his hand thrust into his bosom would become white with leprosy, and water which he would pour upon the ground would become blood; Ex. 4:1-9.
37. Simeon; Luke 2:29-32. The words open the Latin version of the hymn.
38. Saul; 1 Sam. 9:3—10:1.
39. "Joy cometh in the morning"; Ps. 30:5.
40. "For theirs is the kingdom of heaven"; Matt. 5:10-12.
41. By recalling David's eating of the shew-bread; Mark 2:23-26.
42. "Defer not to pay it"; Eccl. 5:4.
43. After his resurrection, when he met seven of them returning from fishing on the Sea of Galilee; John 21:1-13.
44. "Thou shalt not steal"; Ex. 20:15.
45. John 3:16.

SERIES X.—Continued.

46. The region south of the Dead Sea; Edom.
47. He took for himself the spoil of the Canaanites which was devoted to the Lord, and so caused the defeat at Ai; Josh 7:1-23.
48. Ex-high priest at the time of Christ's trial.
49. "But they that deal truly are his delight"; Prov. 12:22.
50. "The Sabbath was made for man"; Mark 2:27.

SERIES XI.

1. Sarah (Sarai); Gen. 11:29, 30.
2. The Lord spoke thus to Moses when the latter protested his lack of eloquence; Ex. 4:10-12.
3. Eli; 1 Sam. 4:18.
4. That it was not to be eaten at all; Lev. 17:10-14.
5. "God sent not his Son into the world to condemn the world"; John 3:17.
6. Cain, after killing Abel; Gen. 4:9.
7. Bethel, Gilgal, and Mizpah; 1 Sam. 7:16.
8. It was followed by a plague; Num. 11:31-34.
9. In Proverbs (3:13-26).
10. Utterly destroy them; Deut. 7:1-3.
11. Solomon; 1 Kings 4:33.
12. Abraham's nephew; Gen. 12:5.
13. Ai; Josh. 8:1-29.
14. By lot; 1 Sam. 10:19-21.
15. The escape of the Jews from the wholesale massacre planned by Haman; Esth. 9:23-32.
16. Jael, wife of Heber, by driving a nail into his temples as he lay asleep; Judg. 4:18-22.
17. In the land of Uz, in the Syrian desert south of Damascus; Job 1:1.
18. David, who wrote "My times are in thy hand," in Ps. 31:15.
19. Ninety feet long, thirty feet wide, forty-five feet high; 1 Kings 6:2.
20. The word means "ten cities," and names a region east of the Sea of Galilee and the Jordan, dominated by ten confederated Greek cities; Matt. 4:25.
21. James and his brother John; Mark 3:17.
22. Near Shechem in central Palestine (Samaria). He read the Law there to the people.
23. Judas Iscariot, "Iscariot" probably meaning "from Kerioth" in southern Judah.
24. Tiberius Cæsar; Luke 3:1.
25. His height; 1 Sam. 10:23.
26. God's people; Isa. 5:1-7.
27. He got into a boat and preached from it; Mark 3:9.
28. She built a room for him to occupy whenever he passed that way; 2 Kings 4:8-10.
29. Because they thought he was beside himself, he roused the multitude to such a pitch of enthusiasm; Mark 3:21.
30. Manasseh; 2 Chron. 33:1-13.
31. Pontius Pilate; Luke 3:1.
32. Because he danced in his rejoicing when the ark was brought to Jerusalem; 1 Chron. 15:29.
33. Simon Peter and Andrew, James and John, Philip and Bartholomew, Matthew and Thomas, James the son of Alphæus and Thaddæus, Simon the Zealot and Judas Iscariot; Mark 3:16-19.
34. Herod Antipas, the "Tetrarch" or "ruler of a fourth" (of the kingdom of Herod the Great).
35. That it "maketh the heart sick"; Prov. 13:12.
36. To the east of it.
37. That every one depends on the farmer; Eccl. 5:9.
38. Because at that age he became a "son of the law," under obligation to attend the feasts in person; Luke 2:41, 42.
39. "Thou shalt not bear false witness against thy neighbor"; Ex. 20:16.
40. In the temptations in the wilderness; Matt. 4:1-4.

SERIES XI.—Continued.

41. Because "their deeds were evil"; John 3:19.
42. The Son of God; Dan. 3:25.
43. It was a place, probably in the Jordan valley, where John baptized because of the many springs; John 3:23.
44. The victory of God's people over their foes; Judg. 5.
45. "Whereby we must be saved"; Acts 4:12.
46. Herod Antipas, because John condemned him publicly for marrying his brother Philip's wife, Herodias; Matt. 14:1-5.
47. "Christ died for us"; Rom. 5:8.
48. That he "hateth his son"; Prov. 13:24.
49. John the Baptist; Luke 3: 7.
50. Andrew and Peter; Matt. 4:18, 19.

SERIES XII.

1. His brother Aaron; Ex. 4:13-16.
2. It flows from the Plain of Esdraelon alongside Mt. Carmel to the Mediterranean. Sisera's army was defeated there, Judg. 4:7; 5:21; and there Elijah slew the priests of Baal; 1 Kings 18:40.
3. "The glory is departed"; 1 Sam. 4:21, 22.
4. To create bread for satisfying his hunger; to cast himself down from the temple pinnacle and so gain a hearing; to worship Satan and thus win the world; Matt. 4:1-11..
5. Ur in Chaldæa; Gen. 11:31.
6. When, at the age of twelve, he tarried in the temple, and was found there by his anxious parents; Luke 2:49.
7. Cain; Gen. 4:13.
8. "He must increase, but I must decrease"; John 3:30.
9. In Mesopotamia. Terah moved there, and from there his son Abraham set out for Canaan; Gen. 11:31.
10. "That shineth more and more unto the perfect day"; Prov. 4:18.
11. Eight; Matt. 5:1-12.
12. They were choked by the thorns; Mark 4:7.
13. The unlawful wife of Herod Antipas, who plotted the death of John the Baptist; Mark 3:19.
14. Seth; Luke 3:38.
15. To Pharaoh, when Moses was trying to get the Israelites out of Egypt; Ex. 5:1.
16. John the Baptist; Luke 3:11.
17. When he preached in Nazareth; Luke 4:24.
18. Moses, speaking of the manna; Deut. 8:3.
19. The district of central Palestine; also a city there, which was the capital of the Northern Kingdom.
20. About thirty years old; Mark 3:23.
21. His nephew, Lot; Gen. 12:4.
22. Peter and John; Acts 4:13.
23. A winnowing fan; Mark 3:17.
24. They were a mixed race, for the Assyrians had sent many colonists thither. Their offer to join in the rebuilding of the temple was contemptuously rejected. They believed only the Pentateuch.
25. From Isaiah; (61:1, 2).
26. From the slave-labor of the Israelites in Egypt; Ex. 5:6-14.
27. "That they may see your good works, and glorify your Father which is in heaven"; Matt. 5:16.
28. Blasphemy against the Holy Spirit; Mark 3:28, 29.
29. A brook in Canaan where the spies cut the great bunch of grapes which they carried off to show the fruitfulness of the land; Num. 13:23, 24.
30. A comparison or little story illustrating moral or religious truth; Mark 4:2.
31. "Thou shalt have no other Gods before me"; Ex. 20:3.
32. The birds devoured them; Mark 4:4.
33. At Sychar in Samaria; John 4:5, 6.

SERIES XII.—Continued.

34. He built an altar there to the Lord; Gen. 12:8.
35. "Whosoever shall do the will of God"; Mark 3:35.
36. People of near-by Gibeon; Josh 9:3.
37. Noon; the day, which was divided into twelve hours, began at sunrise and ended at sunset; John 4:6.
38. When Aaron was confronted with the Egyptian magicians; Ex. 7:10-12.
39. "If a kingdom be divided against itself, that kingdom cannot stand"; Matt. 5:24.
40. Gideon.
41. They were not to reap the corners of their fields or gather their grapes closely, but leave something for the poor; Lev. 19:9, 10.
42. The poor in spirit, the mourners, the meek, the seekers for righteousness, the merciful, the pure in heart, the peacemakers, the persecuted; Matt. 5:1-12.
43. That was the fate of the deceitful people of Gibeon; Josh. 9:21.
44. The poor, the broken-hearted, the captives, the blind, and the bruised; Luke 4:18-21.
45. Because of a famine in Canaan; Gen. 12:10.
46. Christ's; Luke 4:32.
47. They sprang up quickly, but soon withered; Mark 4:5, 6.
48. To punish her for speaking against Moses because he had married an Ethiopian woman; Num. 12:1-15.
49. To salt and to light; Matt. 5:13-16.
50. (1) Water turned to blood; (2) frogs; (3) lice; (4) flies; (5) murrain; (6) boils; (7) hail; (8) locusts; (9) darkness; (10) death of the firstborn; Ex. 7:14—12:30.

SERIES XIII.

1. That of Pharaoh during the ten plagues.
2. For his mercy endureth for ever."
3. John the Baptist, to the soldiers; Mark 3:14.
4. 'Out of it are the issues of life"; Prov. 4:23.
5. In the regions south of Canaan; Num. 13:29.
6. Nebuchadnezzar; Dan. 4:30.
7. The third son of Adam and Eve; Gen. 4:25.
8. Gath, Gaza, Ashdod, Ashkelon, and Ekron; Amos 1:6-8.
9. "For they shall be called the children of God"; Matt. 5:9.
10. Terah; Gen. 11:31.
11. They yielded thirtyfold, sixtyfold, or an hundredfold.
12. The Midianites; Judg. 6:1-11.
13. "Thou shalt not commit adultery"; Ex. 20:14.
14. By "a great fish" (not a whale); Jonah 1:17.
15. "Swear not at all"; Matt. 5:34.
16. Saying that his wife was his sister; Gen. 12:11-20. (She was his half-sister, but that was only part of the truth).
17. "Whosoever shall compel thee to go a mile, go with him twain"; Matt. 5:41.
18. Said by Peter and John when the Sanhedrin bade them stop preaching; Acts 4:18-20.
19. Ps. 119.
20. The parable of the sower; Mark 4:19.
21. John, who arrived first, and Peter, who entered first; John 20:2-10.
22. The plain of the Jordan; Gen. 13:10, 11.
23. His selling a field and contributing the proceeds to the needs of the Jerusalem Christians; Acts 4:36.
24. "With what measure ye mete, it shall be measured to you"; Mark 4:24.
25. Haggai, Zechariah, and Malachi. who wrote the last three Books of the Old Testament.
26. Christ's command just before the great haul of fishes; Luke 5:4.

SERIES XIII.—Continued.

27. Nebuchadnezzar; Dan. 4:33.
28. Christ's conversation at the well of Sychar; John 4:14.
29. In the plain of Mamre, in Hebron; Gen. 13:18.
30. "Grace did much more abound"; Rom. 5:20.
31. Caleb and Joshua; Ex. 13:30; 14:6-9.
32. The servant of Elisha; 2 Kings 4:12.
33. "The end thereof are the ways of death"; Prov. 14:12.
34. "Without blemish, a male of the first year"; Ex. 12:5.
35. "The son of consolation"; Acts 4:36.
36. "Be ye therefore perfect, even as your Father which is in heaven is perfect"; Matt. 5:48.
37. "Worship him in spirit and in truth"; John 4:24.
38. Because of their lack of faith and their despair when the ten spies reported unfavorably; Num. 14:22-24.
39. "He that trusteth in the Lord, mercy shall compass him about"; Ps. 32:10.
40. They were of cedar overlaid with pure gold; 1 Kings 6:16, 21.
41. "The Lord gave, and the Lord hath taken away; blessed be the name of the Lord"; Job. 1:21.
42. Ready to set forth on a journey, their loins girded, shoes on their feet, staff in their hand, and they were to eat it in haste; Ex. 12:11.
43. Fifteen Psalms (120-134) used probably by pilgrims going up to Jerusalem.
44. One of the chief of David's temple singers and musicians; 1 Chron. 16:5.
45. Gibeah; 1 Sam. 10:26.
46. The payment was to be made every night, on the conclusion of the work; Lev. 19:13.
47. Worthless people, "Belial" ("worthlessness") being personified.
48. A year for every day of the spies' exploration of Canaan; Num. 14:34.
49. Peter, after the great haul of fishes; Luke 5:8.
50. A race of giants in southern Canaan; Goliath was probably one of them; Num. 13:28, 33.

SERIES XIV.

1. In the plain of the Jordan near the Dead Sea.
2. To the side posts and lintel of the door; Ex. 12:7.
3. He was stoned to death; Num. 15:32-36.
4. Joses; Acts 4:36.
5. "When thou doest alms, let not thy left hand know what thy right hand doeth"; Matt. 6:3.
6. It was a reminder of God's commandments and of the holiness God requires; Num. 15:37-40.
7. "First the blade, then the ear, after that the full corn in the ear"; Mark 4:28.
8. Chedorlaomer, king of Elam, to whom Sodom and Gomorrah were tributary; Gen. 14:1-12.
9. To the tiny grain of mustard seed; Mark 4:30.
10. Simon Peter; Luke 5:10.
11. The feast of unleavened bread; Ex. 12:17-20.
12. An unnamed leper; Luke 5:12.
13. "When thou prayest, enter into thy closet, and when thou hast shut thy door, pray to thy Father which is in secret"; Matt. 6:6.
14. Not the merit of the Israelites but the wickedness of the Canaanites; Deut. 9:5.
15. A palsied man, name not given; Luke 5:19.
16. The Samaritan woman of Sychar; John 4:26.
17. "He that doeth the will of God abideth for ever"; 1 John 2:17.

SERIES XIV.—Continued.

18. "My meat is to do the will of him that sent me"; John 4:34.
19. Ananias, in the early church of Jerusalem, lied in giving part of the price of a possession to the church, pretending that he was giving the whole; Acts 5:1-4.
20. "Thou shalt not take the name of the Lord thy God in vain"; Ex. 20:7.
21. Solomon's; Acts 5:12.
22. For Gideon, that he might know he had been talking with an angel; Judg. 6:17-24.
23. That the sick were laid where it might fall on them as he passed, expecting it to heal them; Acts 5:15.
24. King of Salem, priest of the most high God, who blessed Abraham; Gen. 14 : 18-20.
25. When an angel opened the prison doors at night and bade the apostles go and preach in the temple; Acts 5:17-23.
26. Jabesh-gilead, saved by Saul; 1 Sam. 11:1-11.
27. "And reverence my sanctuary"; Lev. 19:30.
28. Peter and the other apostles when the Sanhedrin bade them cease preaching Christ; Acts 5:29.
29. That the Israelites might avenge themselves on their enemies; Josh. 10:12-14.
30. The wife of Ananias, who joined him in his lie; Acts 5:7-10.
31. From the Lord's passing over the houses of the Hebrews when going to destroy the firstborn of the Egyptians; Ex. 12:23.
32. By Jacob's well, at Sychar in Samaria; John 4:35.
33. "Thou shalt love thy neighbor as thyself"; Lev. 19:18.
34. "The wages of sin is death"; Rom. 6:23.
35. "That we may obtain mercy, and find grace to help in time of need"; Heb. 4:16.
36. From the Israelites' borrowing of jewels and raiment from them as they left Egypt,—slight wages for their long slavery; Ex. 12:35, 36.
37. "Thou shalt love thy neighbor as thyself"; Jas. 2:8.
38. "Thou shalt love thy neighbor as thyself"; Gal. 5:14.
39. They fled after the battle of Gibeon and hid in a cave, where Joshua and the Israelites captured them by rolling stones against the cave's mouth, afterwards killing the kings and entombing them in the cave; Josh. 10:16-27.
40. Ephesians.
41. Because they themselves were strangers in the land of Egypt; Lev. 19:34.
42. In the Revelation (2:17).
43. The people of Samaria; John 4:42.
44. In Gilgal; 1 Sam. 11:14, 15.
45. In Matthew (6:9-13) and Luke (11:2-4).
46. The law requiring just weights and measures; Lev. 19:35, 36.
47. "There will your heart be also"; Matt. 6:21.
48. Solomon's temple; 1 Kings 6:7.
49. James (2:20).
50. As "the root of all evil"; 1 Tim. 6:10.

SERIES XV.

1. On the island of Cyprus.
2. Abraham; Gen. 15:6.
3. Belshazzar; Dan. 5:1-5.
4. Acacia (shittim); Deut. 10:3.
5. "For they shall obtain mercy"; Matt. 5:7.
6. "O Lord, thou hast searched me and known me"; Ps. 139:1.
7. In connection with Abraham's sleep; Gen. 15:12.
8. Habakkuk (2:4). Paul; Rom. 1:17, etc.

SERIES XV.—Continued.

9. "He that earneth wages earneth wages to put it into a bag wtih holes"; Haggai 1:6.
10. By human sacrifices, especially the burning of children in the fire; Lev. 20:2.
11. God and mammon; Matt. 6:24.
12. They rebelled against Moses, and the earth opened and swallowed them up; Num. 16:1-50.
13. Christ's farewell words to his disciples.
14. Abraham; Gen. 15:17.
15. "Sufficient unto the day is the evil thereof"; Matt. 6:34.
16. When he stilled the tempest; Mark4:39.
17. "The Lamb is the light thereof"; Rev. 21:23.
18. East of the Sea of Galilee; Mark 5:1.
19. Succoth; Ex. 12:37.
20. Driven by Christ into a herd of swine; Mark 5:11-13.
21. Gideon; Judg. 6:25-32.
22. It pictures the cured Gadarene demoniac; Mark 5:15.
23. Four hundred and thirty years; Ex. 12:40.
24. Levi (Matthew); Luke 5:27-29.
25 Samuel; 1 Sam. 12:1.
26. When, on the Sabbath, he healed the man with a withered hand; Luke 6:6-11.
27. Fifteen feet; 1 Kings 6:23-28.
28. Bartholomew; Luke 6:14.
29. Chiefly in being much condensed.
30. He obtained a son for her from the Lord, and when the boy died he brought him back to life; 2 Kings 4:13-37.
31. Healing, from Cana, the son of a nobleman of Capernaum; John 4:46-54.
32. Satan; Job. 2:4.
33. In Jerusalem; John 5:2.
34. The Shunammite woman, when Elisha offered to advance her by gaining the interest of the king; 2 Kings 4:13.
35. Judas, the brother of James, who was probably the same as Lebbæus surnamed Thaddæus; Matt. 10:3; Luke 6:16.
36. High priest under David; 1 Chron. 16:39.
37. A man who had been sick thirty-eight years; John 5:5-9.
38. John the Baptist; John 5:35.
39. "Blessed is the nation whose God is the Lord"; Ps. 33:12.
40. Five barley cakes and two small fishes; John 6:9.
41. "Sin is a reproach to any people"; Prov. 14:34.
42. By having the disciples, after the feeding of the five thousand, gather up the fragments, "that nothing be lost"; John 6:12.
43. When, on the Sabbath, he healed the man at the Pool of Bethesda, and the Jews criticised him for working a cure on that day.
44. "They are increased that eat them"; Eccl. 5:11.
45. A great Jewish rabbi, who saved the apostles when the Sanhedrin sought to kill them; Acts 5:33-40.
46. The apostles found they had no time to attend to the distribution of food among the poor Christians of Jerusalem; Acts 6:1-4.
47. About three pecks, five quarts; Isa. 5:10.
48. Stephen, Philip, Prochorus, Nicanor, Timon, Parmenas, and Nicolas.
49. "Or the leopard his spots?" Jer. 13:23.
50. Twelve baskets full; John 6:13.

SERIES XVI.

1. The Sanhedrin, the highest governing body of the Jews.
2. Hagar, Gen. 16:15.
3. Christ's last prayer with his disciples; John 17.
4. "Abram" means "lofty father" and "Abraham" has the meaning of "father of a multitude," and the change was made just before his son Isaac was born; Gen. 17:5.

SERIES XVI.—Continued.

5. That he was "learned in all the wisdom of the Egyptians"; Acts 7:22.
6. In Leviticus (24:20).
7. One whose hand is against every man and every man's hand against him; Gen. 16:12.
8. Timothy; 1 Tim. 6:12.
9. Because it was a token for Moses, to still the murmurings against him; Num. 17:1-9.
10. Seventy, corresponding to the seventy elders of the days of Moses. The president, the high-priest, made it seventy-one.
11. Blessings from Mt. Gerizim and curses from Mt. Ebal, in Samaria; Deut. 11:29.
12. By the promise of a son in his old age; Gen. 18:1-15.
13. The Christian hope; Heb. 6:19.
14. Because it was fortified by the Egyptians and the hostile Philistines lay athwart it; Ex. 13:17.
15. Hebron; Josh. 14:6-15.
16. Stephen; Acts 6:15.
17. Jerubbaal ("let Baal plead") because he threw down the altar of Baal; Judg. 6:32.
18. Of the power of the tongue; Jas. 3:5.
19. A thunderstorm in the wheat harvest, when such a thing was unknown in Palestine; 1 Sam. 12:16-19.
20. Seven years; 1 Kings 6:38.
21. Forty years in Egypt, forty years in Midian, forty years with the Israelites in the desert.
22. God, speaking to Abraham when a son was promised him in his old age; Gen. 18:14.
23. Hagar; Gen. 16:6, 7.
24. Stephen (Acts 7: 48) and Paul (Acts 17:24).
25. Joseph's; Ex. 13:19.
26. A fleece became wet or dry according to his wish; Judg. 6:36-40.
27. That of Sardis; Rev. 3:1.
28. When he told David to build a temple and was afterwards told by the Lord that David should not build it; 1 Chron. 17:1-15.
29. Eliphaz, Bildad and Zophar.
30. Stephen, by stoning; Acts 7:59.
31. "Saveth such as be of a contrite spirit"; Ps. 34:18.
32. Thirteen years; 1 Kings 7:1.
33. The seraphim attending upon Jehovah; Isa. 6:3.
34. The presence of Jehovah, in a pillar of cloud by day and of fire by night; Ex. 13:21, 22.
35. It discloses the fault-finder, a beam in his own eye while he seeks to remove a mote from his brother's eye; Matt. 7:1-5.
36. He put in meal and it became healthful; 2 Kings 4:38-41.
37. Those who had charge of the synagogue service, especially inviting the speakers; Mark 5:22.
38. "Fear ye not, stand still, and see the salvation of the Lord"; Ex. 14:13.
39. "There the weary be at rest"; Job 3:17.
40. To the crackling of thorns under a pot; Eccl. 7:6.
41. One hundred; and some remained over; 2 Kings 4:42-44.
42. "For they shall be comforted'; Matt. 5:4.
43. A Roman centurion, name unknown; Luke 7:1-5.
44. By praying for his enemies; Acts 7:60; Luke 23:34.
45. After the feeding of the five thousand; John 6:15.
46. "A soft answer turneth away wrath: but grievous words stir up anger"; Prov. 15:1.
47. Saul (Paul); Acts 7:58.
48. "To be spiritually minded is life and peace"; Rom. 8:6.
49. "All things work together for good to them that love God"; Rom. 9:28.
50. "The Lord shall fight for you, and ye shall hold your peace"; Ex. 14:14.

SERIES XVII.

1. "Who can be against us?" Rom. 8:31.
2. With the picture of a virtuous woman; Prov. 31:10-31.
3. By tithes and other offerings; Num. 18:21.
4. "The former days were better than these"; Eccl. 7:10.
5. A Syrian general, who was a leper, healed by bathing in the Jordan at Elisha's command; 2 Kings 5:1-19.
6. "Other foundation can no man lay than that is laid, which is Jesus Christ"; 1 Cor. 3:11.
7. Agur, Prov. 30; and King Lemuel, Prov. 31:1-9.
8. Every seventh year every Hebrew debtor was to be released from his debt; Deut. 15:2.
9. Isaiah; Isa. 6:6.
10. Christ; Eph. 2:14.
11. "The Lord delivereth him out of them all"; Ps. 34:19.
12. The Hebrew captive in Syria who told Naaman's wife about Elisha's miraculous powers; 2 Kings 5:2, 3.
13. Lev. 25:10.
14. Paul, to Timothy; 2 Tim. 1:12.
15. "The fathers have eaten sour grapes, and the children's teeth are set on edge"; Ezek. 18:2.
16. The master thrust an awl through the slave's ear into the door of his house; Deut. 15:16, 17.
17. "Beholding the evil and the good"; Prov. 15:3.
18. "For they shall be filled"; Matt. 5:6.
19. Dan. 5:27,—Daniel's interpretation of the writing on the wall.
20. They were to be released in the seventh year; Num. 15:12.
21. He threw them back at the chief priests and elders, and they used them to buy the potter's field, to bury strangers in; Matt. 27:3-10.
22. "Ye ask, and receive not, because ye ask amiss"; Jas. 4:3.
23. In the reign of Josiah, by the high priest Hilkiah; 2 Kings 22:1-11.
24. To shelter from the blood avenger any one who killed another unawares and unwittingly; Josh. 20:1-6.
25. "And desperately wicked"; Jer. 17:9.
26. Laodicea; Rev. 3:16.
27. In the Sermon on the Mount; Matt. 7:6.
28. Kadesh in Galilee, Shechem in Samaria, Hebron in Judah; and, on the east of Jordan, Golan in the north, Ramoth in the center (Gilead), and Bezer in the south; Josh. 20:7-9.
29. It should be "strait and narrow"; Matt. 7:14.
30. 150 feet; 1 Kings 7:2.
31. Philadelphia; Rev. 3:7, 8.
32. The ruler of the synagogue whose little daughter Jesus raised from the dead; Mark 6:22-43.
33. By not waiting for Samuel at Gilgal, but offering sacrifice himself; 1 Sam. 13:5-14.
34. "It shall die"; Ezek. 18:20.
35. Abraham, in pleading for the cities of the plain; Gen. 18:25.
36. Because the centurion humbly asked Christ to heal his servant without going to his house; Luke 7:1-10.
37. Gideon, conqueror of the Midianites; Judg. 7:1-8.
38. Peter, James, and John; Mark 5:37.
39. Hiram of Tyre (not to be confounded with King Hiram of Tyre); 1 Kings 7:13, 14.
40. "Than a stalled ox and hatred therewith"; Prov. 15:17.
41. Jehovah, to Moses, before the crossing of the Red Sea; Ex. 14:15.
42. In Galilee, five miles from Nazareth.
43. Walking to them on the sea in the storm; John 6:20.
44. They were to lie fallow every seventh year; Lev. 25:1-7.
45. David; Ps. 36:9.
46. To the dead daughter of Jaïrus; Mark 5:41.
47. Every fiftieth year, when the land was to lie fallow and every one was to return to his possession; Lev. 25:8-17.

SERIES XVII.—Continued.

48. Jachin (on the right) and Boaz (on the left), perhaps meaning "firmness" and "strength"; 1 Kings 7:21.
49. To the dead son of the widow of Nain; Luke 7:14.
50. Sodom and Gomorrah; Gen. 18:20-33.

SERIES XVIII.

1. In connection with the feeding of the five thousand; John 6:27.
2. The northern portion of the Gulf of Suez.
3. Three times: at the passover (the feast of unleavened bread), at the feast of weeks (Pentecost), and at the feast of tabernacles; Deut. 16:16.
4. "He ever liveth to make intercession for them"; Heb. 7:25.
5. "Thou shalt not wrest judgment; thou shalt not respect persons, neither take a gift"; Deut. 16:19.
6. On the east of the Jordan, by the two and a half tribes that settled there, not for sacrifice but as a witness that they adhered to the worship of Jehovah; Josh. 22:1-34.
7. Moses; Ex. 15:1-19.
8. It was the warcry of Gideon's three hundred as they overcame the host of the Midianites; Judg. 7:20.
9. "That ye believe on him whom he hath sent"; John 6:29.
10. Only the two tables of stone on which the Ten Commandments were inscribed; 1 Kings 8:9.
11. Miriam; Ex. 15:20, 21.
12. When the Lord was angry with David because he numbered the people; 1 Chron. 21:1-16.
13. "Giveth grace unto the humble"; Jas. 4:6.
14. "I am the bread of life"; John 6:35.
15. "There is no restraint to the Lord to save by many or by few"; 1 Sam. 14:6.
16. Abana and Pharpar, rivers of Damascus; 2 Kings 5:12.
17. Philip; Acts 8:5-8.
18. The prayer of Solomon at the dedication of the temple; 1 Kings 8:22-53.
19. They were bitter, but were miraculously sweetened; Ex. 15:23-26.
20. Joab; 1 Chron. 20:1, and many other references.
21. In Samaria, converted by Philip; Acts 8:9-13.
22. At Gath, being a son of Goliath; 1 Chron. 20:6.
23. They blew their trumpets, smashed their pitchers, and waved the torches which had been concealed by the pitchers; Judg. 7:16-20.
24. Where Moses drew water from a rock; Num. 20:12, 13.
25. Because he tried to buy the gift of the Holy Spirit; Acts 8:18-24.
26. "As the sparks fly upward'; Job. 5:7.
27. Peter, in rebuking Simon of Samaria; Acts 8:23.
28. "Is better than the riches of many wicked"; Ps. 37:16.
29. It was an oasis, with twelve walls and seventy palm trees, where the Israelites camped after leaving Egypt; Ex. 15:27.
30. By climbing up a cliff and falling upon them suddenly; 1 Sam. 14:7-23.
31. "We are more than conquerors"; Rom. 9:37.
32. From Eccl. 7:29: "God hath made man upright, but they have sought out many inventions."
33. That land should not be permanently alienated; Lev. 25:23.
34. Paul, in 1 Cor. 3:16.
35. In Isaiah (7:14).
36. "And an haughty spirit before a fall"; Prov. 16:18.
37. Paul, because he had persecuted the church; Eph. 3:8.
38. Timothy; 1 Tim. 2:3.
39. Isaiah's second son, whose name, meaning "spoil speedeth, prey hasteth," was given as a prophecy of the victory of the Assyrians; Isa. 8:1-4.

SERIES XVIII.—Continued.

40. No Jew was to take interest from another Jew; Lev. 25:35-38.
41. Jeremiah (17:21-27).
42. Rev. 3:20.
43. Daniel, because he would not cease praying to Jehovah; Dan. 6:1-28.
44. In Kadesh-barnea; Num. 20:1.
45. In Amos (4:12).
46. Lot obtained its preservation from the angels on the ground that it was only "a little one"; Gen. 19:17-23.
47. Nineveh; Jonah 3:4-10.
48. He did not honor God, but spoke as if he were working the miracle in his own power; Num. 20:10, 11.
49. Habakkuk (2:15).
50. Because she looked backward in escaping from Sodom; Gen. 19:26.

SERIES XIX.

1. Haggai (2:7).
2. Jesus, concerning false teachers; Matt. 7:16.
3. Saul's vision of Christ near Damascus; Acts 9:5.
4. The Lord of hosts, *i. e.,* of armies; Rom. 9:29.
5. In unbelieving Nazareth; Mark 6:1-6.
6. Paul; Eph. 4:5.
7. Timothy; 2 Tim. 2:15.
8. He sent them forth two and two; Mark 6:7.
9. The ten tables of the shewbread, the altar of incense, and the ten golden candlesticks; Heb. 9:2-4. The altar of incense really belonged in the Most Holy Place, as Hebrews says.
10. Jesus, concerning false teachers; Matt. 7:20.
11. The ark of the covenant, with the tables of the Law, and (probably beside it) the pot of manna and Aaron's rod that budded; Heb. 9:4.
12. The daughter of Herodias, who asked for the head of John the Baptist as a reward for her dancing; Mark 6:17-29.
13. "And he will flee from you"; Jas. 4:7.
14. The prayers of saints; Rev. 5:8.
15. When his ways were contrasted with those of John the Baptist; Luke 7:31-35.
16. Whatever was gathered, it exactly met the need of the gatherer; Ex. 16:18.
17. When the woman who was a sinner anointed his feet with costly ointment; Luke 7:36-50.
18. To the lands of King Abimelech; Gen. 20:1-18.
19. At Mount Horeb; Ex. 17:1-7.
20. The parable of the houses on the rock and on the sand; Matt. 7:24-27.
21. The refusal of the Edomites to let the Israelites pass through their territory on the way to Canaan; Num. 20:14-21.
22. Two or three witnesses were required, and the witnesses were to cast the first stones in the execution; Deut. 17:6, 7.
23. He entertained Christ at a meal, but did not receive him with ordinary courtesy; Luke 7:44-47.
24. It did not fall on the Sabbath, but the day before the Sabbath a double supply was gathered, and this extra supply did not become corrupt; Ex. 16:19-30.
25. Isaac; Gen. 21:1-8.
26. John the Baptist, whom he had beheaded, come back from the grave; Mark 6:16.
27. "The bread that I will give is my flesh, which I will give for the life of the world"; John 6:51.
28. At Shechem; Josh. 24:1.
29. On Mount Hor; Num. 20:22-29.
30. Peter; John 6:68.
31. Like wafers made with honey; Ex. 16:31.
32. By Joshua, in his farewell address; Josh 24:15.
33. On the last day of the feast of tabernacles; John 7:37.
34. Ishmael, son of Hagar; Gen. 21:9-21.
35. The Amalekites; Ex. 17:8.

SERIES XIX.—Continued.

36. Officers sent by the Pharisees and chief priests to arrest Jesus; John 7:45, 46.
37. In Shechem, in Jacob's field; Josh. 24:32.
38. Spoken of Gideon and his three hundred in their long pursuit of the defeated Midianites; Judg. 8:4.
39. Because Jonathan, not hearing his father's command that all the host should fast, had eaten a little honey; and the people interceded for the prince; 1 Sam. 14:24-45.
40. Nicodemus; John 7:50-53.
41. Agag, king of the Amalekites; 1 Sam. 15:1-35.
42. His son Eleazar; Num. 20:26-28.
43. Candace; Acts 8:27.
44. He sat on a hill and held up his hands in prayer, Aaron and Hur holding up his hands; Ex. 17:9-16.
45. The last king of Judah, Zedekiah; 2 Kings 25:7.
46. Isaiah (53:7, 8); Philip; Acts 8:27-38.
47. Samuel, to Saul; 1 Sam. 15:22.
48. Samuel; 1 Sam. 15:29.
49. Damascus; Acts 9:1, 2.
50. Bread from heaven given to feed the Israelites during their forty years of wandering in the wilderness; Ex. 16:1-15.

SERIES XX.

1. Because he took from Naaman the payment for his cure which Elisha had refused; 2 Kings 5:20-27.
2. That all secrets shall some day be disclosed; Luke 8:16.
3. Jemina, Keziah, and Keren-happuch. Job 42:14, 15.
4. When they brought to him a woman taken in adultery; John 8:3-6.
5. He healed two demoniacs; Matt. 8:28; Luke 8:27.
6. "Let them lead me"; Ps. 43:3.
7. "He that is without sin among you, let him first cast a stone at her"; John 8:7-11.
8. It means going through the form of worship for the sake of policy, as Naaman proposed to do; 2 Kings 5:17-19.
9. "Light"; John 8:12.
10. East of the Sea of Galilee; Luke 8:26.
11. "The end thereof are the ways of death"; Prov. 16:25.
12. "I do always those things that please him" (the Father); John 8:29.
13. "A dead lion"; Eccl. 9:4.
14. One lied about his gift to the church (Acts 5:1-6); the other was sent to Saul to restore his sight (Acts 9:10-18).
15. Isaiah (9:6).
16. Judas Iscariot; the other Judas who was an apostle; the Judas who led a revolt (Acts 5:37); Judas (Jude), the Lord's brother, author of the Epistle; Judas of Damascus with whom Saul stayed (Acts 9:11); Judas Barsabbas, delegate to Antioch (Acts 15:22).
17. The Gadarene demoniac; Luke 8:30.
18. Jeremiah; see Jer. 18:1-6, etc.
19. It is a leading street in Damascus; Saul stayed there in the house of Judas (Acts 9:11).
20. Saul of Tarsus; Acts 9:15.
21. Hosea (1:1).
22. Barnabas; Acts 9:26, 27.
23. Tarsus, in Cilicia, at the northeastern corner of the Mediterranean.
24. Amos (6:4).
25. The Gadarene demoniac; Luke 8:31-33.
26. At Lydda; Æneas; Acts 9:32-35.
27. Isaiah (2:4) and Micah (4:3, 4).
28. In Joppa, Palestine's one seaport; Acts 9:36.
29. To confess Jesus and believe in his resurrection; Rom. 10:9.
30. "Let all the earth keep silence before him"; Hab. 2:20.
31. Tabitha; Acts 9:36.
32. "A certain scribe"; Matt. 8:19.

SERIES XX.—Continued.

33. "Foolishness with God"; 1 Cor. 3:19.
34. Second John; 2 John 1.
35. "All scripture is given by inspiration of God," etc.; 2 Tim. 3:16.
36. Peter; 2 Pet. 1:5-7.
37. When a scribe said that he would follow Christ wherever he went; Matt. 8:19, 20.
38. That she is "full of good works and alms deeds"; Acts 9:36.
39. In Revelation (6:8).
40. It is the hill in Jerusalem on which the temple was built.
41. When some one said that he would follow Jesus, but first he would attend his father's funeral; Matt. 8:21, 22.
42. That he should appoint judges and delegate his judicial work to them; Ex. 18:13-26.
43. Not the things from without, but the things from within the man; Mark 7:15.
44. "He shall give his angels charge over thee, to keep thee in all thy ways"; Ps. 91:11.
45. When he went northward for a rest, but a miracle was sought from him; Mark 7:24.
46. "Tabitha, arise"; Acts 9:40.
47. On a mount in "the land of Moriah," probably the hill on which Solomon built his temple; Gen. 22:2.
48. The Syro-Phœnician, with her saying about the dogs under the table; Mark 7:25-30.
49. An officer of Sennacherib who tried to win over the people of Jerusalem.
50. Mary Magdalene; Luke 8:2.

SERIES XXI.

1. King Hezekiah and the prophet Isaiah; Isa. 38:1-8.
2. A family who were loyal to the command of an ancestor that they should drink no wine nor dwell in houses; Jeremiah used them as an example for the unfaithful men of Judah; Jer. 35:1-19.
3. She went to Pilate warning him not to condemn Christ, who was a just man, and telling of a dream she had had about Christ; Matt. 27:19.
4. Gideon; Judg. 8:22, 23.
5. When Samuel was ready to anoint Eliab king because of his stately appearance; 1 Sam. 16:6, 7.
6. The priest of Bethel who tried to drive Amos away; Amos 7:10-13.
7. With Simon, a tanner; Acts 9:43.
8. Perhaps in India, probably in southern Arabia; 1 Kings 9:26-28.
9. The value of one lost soul in the eyes of God; Luke 15:1-7.
10. When the king was seized with melancholia, David was sent for, to play on the harp for him; 1 Sam. 16:14-23.
11. "The Lord knoweth them that are his"; 2 Tim. 2:19.
12. Elisha; 2 Kings 6:1-7.
13. Heb. 11.
14. In Deuteronomy (18:15).
15. He said, when the woman was healed by touching the hem of his garment, "I perceive that virtue is gone out of me"; Luke 8:40.
16. "Blue, and purple, and crimson, and fine linen, and wrought cherubims thereon"; 2 Chron. 3:14.
17. "And take up his cross daily, and follow me"; Luke 9:23.
18. To Peter, when he protested against the voice from heaven bidding him eat of the unclean animals let down from heaven; Acts 10:15.
19. "And not to please ourselves"; Rom. 15:1.
20. "Shall be saved"; Rom. 10:13.
21. Herod Antipas; Luke 9:9.
22. In the Psalms; Ps. 45:1.
23. Peter in Cæsarea, Acts 10:26; and Paul in Lystra, Acts 14:13-15.
24. The healing of the deaf man with an impediment in his speech; Mark 7:37.
25. It is based on a saying of Job's; see Job 7:16.

SERIES XXI.—Continued.

26. "Apollos, or Cephas, or the world, or life, or death, or things present, or things to come; all are yours; and ye are Christ's; and Christ is God's"; 1 Cor. 3:21-23.
27. He did so before the feeding of the five thousand (Luke 9:16); he was known to the two of Emmaus by that act (Luke 24:35).
28. Amos; see Amos 7:14, 15.
29. The deaf man with an impediment in his speech; Mark 7:31-36.
30. In Proverbs (16:32).
31. Of Abel; Heb. 11:4.
32. That of Zechariah.
33. "He will draw nigh to you"; Jas. 4:8.
34. A Christian woman from Cenchrea, a seaport of Corinth, whom Paul commended earnestly to the church in Rome; Rom. 16:1.
35. "The spirit giveth life"; 2 Cor. 3:6.
36. In Micah (5:2).
37. The Song of Solomon.
38. In Rev. 7:9-17.
39. Twelve years; Matt. 9:20.
40. In Isaiah (11:1-12).
41. The word means "the valley of Hinnom" (south of Jerusalem), where, on the high places named Topheth, children were sacrificed by fire to Molech, and where, perhaps, offal was burned; so it became a name of hell.
42. Christ, who added, "He is a liar, and the father of it"; John 8:44.
43. Ezekiel's account of Tyre; Ezek. 27:1-36.
44. A centurion of the Italian cohort, living in Cæsarea; Acts 10:1.
45. Isaiah (11:6).
46. Hebrew, Abaddon; Greek, Apollyon; Rev. 9:11.
47. "Before Abraham was, I am"; John 8:58.
48. Paul's secretary, to whom the apostle dictated the Epistle to the Romans; Rom. 16:22.
49. Christ said it to believing Jews, who had been boasting of their freedom from bondage; John 8:36.
50. The valley of Achor ("Troubling") is the valley near Jericho where Achan was stoned to death (Josh. 7:24-26); it is to change its significance entirely; Hos. 2:15.

SERIES XXII.

1. The answer made by Amos to Amaziah; Amos 7:14.
2. When he said, "Before Abraham was, I am"; John 8:58, 59.
3. When he saw the favor in which Cornelius, the Roman centurion, was held by God; Acts 10:34.
4. Paul; Rom. 10:14.
5. A ram caught in a thicket by his horns; Gen. 22:13.
6. Ps. 46:10.
7. Jeremiah; Jer. 20:1-6.
8. Just before opening the eyes of the man born blind; John 9:4.
9. Barnabas; Acts. 11:22.
10. The name means "the Lord will provide"; it is the place where the Lord provided a ram to take the place of the sacrifice of Isaac; Gen. 22:14.
11. Titus; Titus 1:4, 5.
12. "Yesterday, and to-day, and forever"; Heb. 13:8.
13. "A brother is born for adversity"; Prov. 17:17.
14. In Solomon's Song 2:1.
15. Machpelah, the cave beneath the great mosque at Hebron. There were buried Abraham and Sarah, Isaac and Rebekah, Jacob and Leah; Gen. 23:1-20.
16. "To do justly, and to love mercy, and to walk humbly with thy God"; Mic. 6:8.
17. Two blind men of Capernaum; Matt. 9:27-31.
18. "The harvest truly is plenteous, but the laborers are few"; Matt. 9:36-38.

SERIES XXII.—Continued.

19. By her kindness in giving water to him and to his camels; Gen. 24:1-27.
20. Simon Peter and Simon the Canaanite (Cananæan, Zealot); Matt. 10:2, 4.
21. The healing of the blind man of Bethsaida, who at first saw men as trees, walking; Mark 8:24.
22. The Lord said it to Moses, speaking of his guidance of the Israelites from Egypt to Sinai; Ex. 19:4.
23. "Whosoever will save his life shall lose it; but whosoever will lose his life for my sake, the same shall save it"; Luke 9:24.
24. Zech. 4:6.
25. The king of Moab, who was terrified at the approach of the Israelites on their way to Canaan; Num. 22:1-7.
26. Proverbs (17:22).
27. Jeremiah; Jer. 20:14-18.
28. A prophet who lived on the Euphrates, whom the king of Moab tried to get to curse the Israelites, but in vain; Num. 22:1—24:25.
29. "Thou shalt not remove thy neighbor's landmark"; Deut. 19:14.
30. Antioch of Syria.
31. He killed seventy of his brothers and reigned as king; Judg. 9:1-57.
32. The disciples were first called Christians there; Acts 11:26. From there the first foreign missionaries set out; Acts 13:1-4.
33. She saw the angel of the Lord opposing her master's way, and spoke to the prophet; Num. 22:22-31.
34. That he be stoned to death; Deut. 22:18-21.
35. Agabus; Acts 11:27, 28.
36. Our bodies; Rom. 12:1.
37. The prophet Balaam; Num. 24:17-19.
38. "That a man be found faithful"; 1 Cor. 4:2.
39. The one son of Gideon whom Abimelech failed to kill, and who uttered a prophecy of doom upon his brother, the fable of the trees and the bramble; Judg. 9:7-21.
40. Nine feet, nine inches; 1 Sam. 17:4.
41. "A very present help in trouble"; Ps. 46:1.
42. In southwestern Arabia; its queen journeyed far to learn the wisdom of Solomon; 1 Kings 10:1-13.
43. Decreasing the measure and increasing the price; Amos 8:5.
44. At Dothan; 2 Kings 6:8-17.
45. Of such a man he himself would be ashamed in his glorious return; Luke 9:26.
46. Rehoboam; 2 Chron. 10:1.
47. Just before opening the eyes of the man born blind; John 9:5.
48. The Babylonian name of Zerubbabel, whom Cyrus allowed to lead a return of the Hebrews to Palestine, making him governor of Jerusalem; Ezra 1:1-11.
49. Job; see Job 9:33.
50. Elisha, surrounded by hostile Syrians, speaking to his terrified servant; 2 Kings 6:13-16.

SERIES XXIII.

1. Peter, in the house of Cornelius; Acts 10:38.
2. "Hearing by the word of God"; Rom. 10:17.
3. Gen. 24:27; said by Abraham's servant on finding Rebekah for a wife for Isaac.
4. It is the seacoast region between Joppa and Mt. Carmel; Solomon's Song 2:1.
5. Hosea (4:17).
6. To drop our sins and assume Christ's righteousness; Eph. 4:22-24.
7. Laban; Gen. 24:29.
8. "Death and life are in the power of the tongue"; Prov. 18:21.
9. Timothy; 2 Tim. 4:2.
10. Mount Sinai, during the giving of the Law; Ex. 19:12.
11. Solomon's Song 2:4.
12. "That he is a rewarder of them that diligently seek him"; Heb. 11:6.

SERIES XXIII.—Continued.

13. Son of Eleazar the high priest and grandson of Aaron; he "made an atonement for the children of Israel"; Num. 25:10-13.
14. Hosea (6:3).
15. James (4:8).
16. Judges of Israel; Judg. 10:1-5.
17. Obadiah.
18. "The kingdoms of our Lord, and of his Christ; and he shall reign for ever and ever"; Rev. 11:15.
19. Zechariah (4:10); he was a prophet of the return, when the Jews began again in great poverty.
20. Seven; 1 Sam. 17:12.
21. Serpents, doves; Matt. 10:16.
22. On the western shore of the Sea of Galilee; Mark 8:10.
23. Jesse; 1 Sam. 17:12.
24. Sixty-six. Old Testament, 39; New Testament, 3x9, or 27.
25. When they should be brought before rulers and judges; Matt. 10:19.
26. One thousand,—three hundred of them being concubines; 1 Kings 11:3.
27. At the foot of Mt. Hermon; Mark 8:27.
28. James the brother of John; put to death by Herod the king (Agrippa I.); Acts 12:1, 2.
29. Blinded it and led it to Samaria; then he freed it; 2 Kings 6:18-23.
30. When Christ foretold his crucifixion; Mark 9:31, 32.
31. One of Solomon's officers who became king of the Northern Kingdom.
32. "The Lord God is a sun and shield: the Lord will give grace and glory: no good thing will he withhold from them that walk uprightly"; Ps. 84:11.
33. The high priest who returned with Zerrubbabel in the first return from exile; Ezra 3:2.
34. "Cleave to that which is good"; Rom. 12:9.
35. Father of Jeroboam.
36. When Peter rebuked Christ for prophesying his crucifixion; Mark 8:33.
37. Zophar, friend of Job, asked this of the patriarch; Job. 11:7-9.
38. "Word," "power"; 1 Cor. 4:20.
39. "Our guide even unto death"; Ps. 48:14.
40. Satan; Rev. 12:9.
41. It is in the southern part of Jerusalem, and there the man blind from birth washed and received his sight; John 9:6, 7.
42. At the transfiguraton, Luke 9:32; and in the Garden of Gethsemane, Luke 22:45.
43. One of Abraham's wives; Gen. 25:1.
44. The fifth; Ex. 20:12.
45. "Be ye angry, and sin not; let not the sun go down upon your wrath"; Eph. 4:26.
46. At the transfiguration; Luke 9:33.
47. Their father had no sons, but they pleaded their cause before Moses and obtained their father's possessions; Num. 27:1-8.
48. Abraham, the sojourner; Heb. 11:10.
49. "To him it is sin"; Jas. 4:17.
50. Paul; 2 Tim. 4:3.

SERIES XXIV.

1. Hebrews.
2. "All tears from their eyes"; Rev. 21:4.
3. "Thou shalt not muzzle the ox when he treadeth out the corn"; Deut. 25:4.
4. The husband of Naomi, who went from Bethlehem to Moab in time of famine; Ruth 1:1.
5. A squad of four soldiers; Acts 12:4.
6. In the valley of Elah; 1 Sam. 17:19.
7. Peter, in the house of Cornelius; Acts 10:43.
8. By an angel. who opened the prison doors; Acts 12:6-9.
9. David; 1 Sam. 17:37.
10. "Preferring one another"; Rom. 12:10.
11. A fortress in Jerusalem, built by Solomon; 1 Kings 11:27.

SERIES XXIV.—Continued.

12. He was writing about the contagion of evil from a bad man in the Corinthian church; 1 Cor. 5:6.
13. Ben-hadad; 2 Kings 6:24.
14. The Revelation.
15. Rehoboam; 2 Chron. 10:13, 14.
16. "I have fought a good fight, I have finished my course, I have kept the faith"; 2 Tim. 4:7.
17. The first three, because they give synopses of Christ's life.
18. Because it was so sadly inferior to Solomon's temple; Ezra 3:12.
19. Those of the autumn and the spring; Jas. 5:7.
20. 3 John (verse 1).
21. Job, to his comforting (?) friends; Job 12:1.
22. Paul; Eph. 5:16.
23. "Renew a right spirit within me"; Ps. 51:10.
24. Because when he was born his hand had hold of the heel of his twin brother, Esau; Gen. 25:26.
25. Because he was covered with red hair; Gen. 25:25.
26. "A man that hath friends must show himself friendly"; Prov. 18:24.
27. Psalm 51.
28. "Thou shalt not follow a multitude to do evil"; Ex. 23:2.
29. "Thou shalt take no gift: for the gift blindeth the wise"; Ex. 23:8.
30. In the Song of Solomon (2:15).
31. Deut. 28.
32. Jephthah's army made the fugitives from their war with Ephraim pronounce the word, and if they pronounced it "Sibboleth" they were Ephraimites and were slain; Judg. 12:4-6.
33. "Reap the whirlwind"; Hos. 8:7.
34. Mahlon who married Ruth and Chilion who married Orpah; Ruth 1:2, 4.
35. David, before he overthrew Goliath; 1 Sam. 17:47.
36. Said to the Edomites by Obadiah (verse 4).
37. Rehoboam; 1 Kings 12:10.
38. That the Syrian host had vanished; 2 Kings 7:3-11.
39. That not one of them should fall to the ground without our Father; Matt. 11:29.
40. When the Northern Kingdom (Israel) separated from the Southern; 2 Chron. 10:16.
41. "He shall gain the whole world, and lose his own soul"; Mark 8:36.
42. He would not let the Samaritans join him in building the temple, and in revenge they obtained the command of Artaxerxes that the work should cease; Ezra 4:1-24.
43. Job, in the midst of his woes; Job 13:15.
44. When the lad with a dumb spirit was brought to him; Mark 8:14-23.
45. "There is no God"; Ps. 53:1.
46. "He that hath pity upon the poor"; Prov. 19:17.
47. By taking a little child and saying that whoever should receive him in Christ's name was receiving Christ; Luke 9:48.
48. A man who loved "to have the preeminence"; 3 John 9.
49. 1 John.
50. To the door; John 10:1-9.

SERIES XXV.

1. The flight into Egypt of Joseph and Mary with the infant Jesus; Hos. 11:1.
2. "The very hairs of your head are all numbered"; Matt. 10:30.
3. Herold Agrippa I.; Acts 12:20-23.
4. Baruch; Jer. 36:4.
5. Zechariah (8:5).
6. One of Paul's friends who forsook him in his last imprisonment, "having loved this present world"; 2 Tim. 4:10.
7. Moses; Heb. 11:27.
8. Saul and Barnabas; Acts 13:1-3.

SERIES XXV.—Continued.

9. James (5:16).
10. Hosea (11:4).
11. That he in turn would confess or deny them before his Father in heaven; Matt. 10:32.
12. Two.
13. Paul; 1 Thess. 5:22.
14. "A sword"; Matt. 10:34.
15. Peter; 1 Pet. 1:8.
16. To his brother Jacob for a soup of red lentiles; Gen. 25:29-34.
17. The father of the demoniac boy; Mark 9:24.
18. In that of Mary, the mother of John Mark; Acts 12:12.
19. As the wells he dug were taken from him, he moved on and dug others; Gen. 26:17-22.
20. Antioch of Syria; Acts 13:1.
21. In the Revelation (14:13).
22. In the blessing of Moses; Deut. 33:1, 25.
23. The damsel who went to the door of Mary's house to admit Peter, just released from prison; Acts 12:13-15.
24. "This kind can come forth by nothing, but by prayer and fasting"; Mark 9:29.
25. The seaport of Antioch; Acts 13:4.
26. It was the lid of the ark, hiding the tables of the Law from the Presence of God above it, and so typifying the divine mercy; Ex. 25:17-22.
27. He went to live at Cæsarea; Acts 12:19.
28. His disciples had been disputing who should be greatest; Mark 9:33-35.
29. The names of the twelve tribes, which were thus presented before God for his favor; Ex. 28:15-21.
30. In the island of Cyprus, and in the city of Salamis; Acts 13.
31. His disciples had forbidden one who was not of Christ's followers and yet was casting out devils in his name; Christ said, "Forbid him not"; Luke 9:49, 50.
32. By covering his hands and neck with goat skin and pretending to be the hairy Esau; Gen. 27:6-40.
33. Jeohoiakim, king of Judah; Jer. 36: 22-24.
34. They asked Christ for power to bring down fire from heaven on the village, like Elijah; but Christ refused; Luke 9:51-56.
35. God himself, in the land of Moab, but no one knows exactly where; Deut. 34:5, 6.
36. Judges of Israel; Judg. 12:8-15.
37. "The good shepherd giveth his life for the sheep"; John 10:11.
38. John Mark, usually called simply Mark; Acts 13:5.
39. With his sling and five smooth pebbles from a brook; 1 Sam. 17:39, 40.
40. "There shall be one fold, and one shepherd"; John 10:16.
41. The officer in charge of the king's taxes, sent by Rehoboam to the rebellious tribes and by them stoned to death; 1 Kings 12:18.
42. In the synagogues of the Jews; Acts 13:5, etc.
43. Abner; 1 Sam. 17:55.
44. Jehu, the son of Nimshi; 2 Kings 9:20.
45. "I have power to lay it" (his life) "down, and I have power to take it again"; John 10:18.
46. His second letter to Timothy.
47. Orpah returned and Ruth went with Naomi; Ruth 1:7-14.
48. In Romans (12:20).
49. In the blessing of Moses; Deut. 33:1, 27.
50. "That I might by all means save some"; 1 Cor. 9:22.

SERIES XXVI.

1. The king of Egypt who defeated Rehoboam and despoiled the temple and the royal palace; 2 Chron. 12:1-16.
2. Giving a cup of cold water to "one of these little ones"; Matt. 10:42.
3. Haggai and Zechariah; Ezra 5:1, 2.
4. "My yoke is easy, and my burden is light"; Matt. 11:30.
5. Job (14:1).
6. "What God hath joined together, let not man put asunder"; Mark 10:9.
7. "For then would I fly away, and be at rest"; Ps. 55:6.
8. "Of such is the kingdom of God"; Mark 10:14.
9. Proverbs (20:1).
10. The rich young ruler; Mark 10:21.
11. Solomon's Song (5:10).
12. Job (14:14).
13. Disciples sent out by Christ to do evangelistic work after he had sent out the Twelve; Luke 10:1.
14. "Thou wilt keep him in perfect peace, whose mind is stayed on thee"; Isa. 26:3.
15. The parable of the good Samaritan; Luke 10:25-37.
16. Jeremiah; Jer. 32:1-15.
17. A feast (held in November) to celebrate the rededication of the temple after the Greeks had desecrated it for three years by their idolatries; John 10:22.
18. "I and my Father are one"; John 10:30.
19. Ezekiel; Ezek. 37:1-14.
20. The rich young ruler, whom Christ urged to give all he had to the poor, take up his cross, and follow him; Mark 10:21.
21. Didymus, a Greek word meaning "a twin"; "Thomas" is from a Hebrew word of the same meaning; John 11:16.
22. Zechariah (9:9).
23. He was the sorcerer, of Paphos in Cyprus, who was blinded because he opposed Paul; Acts 13:6-11. His other name was Bar-jesus.
24. Martha, Mary, and Lazarus of Bethany; John 11:5.
25. He spoke to Martha, and about Mary, who had chosen "that good part"; Luke 10:38-42.
26. When he began his first missionary tour, in Cyprus; Acts 13:9.
27. Rom. 13:1: "The powers that be are ordained of God."
28. 1 Cor. 11:23-26.
29. Solomon's Song (6:10).
30. "Only Luke is with me"; 2 Tim. 4:11.
31. In Bethany, on the Mount of Olives.
32. To Padan-aram, on the upper Euphrates; Gen. 28:2.
33. Ephesians (6:11-18).
34. "Holiness to the Lord"; Ex. 28:36.
35. Zech. 9:12.
36. Philippians.
37. At Bethel, which means, "the house of God"; Gen. 28:19.
38. Some one who did Paul "much evil," of whom, in his last letter, he bade Timothy beware; 2 Tim. 4:14.
39. Samson; Judg. 13:5.
40. The heroes of faith named in the preceding verses of the chapter; Heb. 11:38.
41. Boaz; Ruth 2:1—4:22.
42. Jeroboam; 1 Kings 12:20.
43. Peter; 1 Pet. 3:7.
44. Michal, daughter of Saul; 1 Sam. 18:20, 27.
45. The world war before the great day of God; Rev. 16:16.
46. Bethel in the south, Dan in the north; 1 Kings 12:28, 29.
47. Jehu; 2 Kings 9:30-37.
48. 1 Pet. 3:19.
49. The father of Samson; Judg. 13:2, 24.
50. That of Jacob at Bethel; Gen. 28:20-22.

SERIES XXVII.

1. In his conversation with the rich young ruler; Mark 10:23-25.
2. Lazarus of Bethany, John 11:1; Lazarus the beggar, Luke 16:20.
3. The deputy of Cyprus, won to Christianity by Paul; Acts 13:7, 12.
4. "Jealousy is cruel as the grave"; Solomon's Song 8:6.
5. The seventy disciples; Luke 10:3.
6. In Ruth (1:16, 17).
7. One of the good kings of Judah, who honored Jehovah; 2 Chron. 14:1-8.
8. The parable of the Good Samaritan, spoken to a lawyer who was testing him; Luke 10:25, 37.
9. The priest and scribe whom King Artaxerxes sent to Jerusalem with rich gifts and a letter of authority; Ezra 7:1-28.
10. Job (19:20).
11. Malachi, meaning "my messenger," a meaning referred to in Mal. 3:1.
12. 'That is higher than I"; Ps. 61:2.
13. Jonah's three days in the body of the great fish; Matt. 12:40.
14. The Ethiopian general whom Asa defeated; 2 Chron. 14:9-15.
15. "Spake often one to another"; Mal. 3:16.
16. The long journey taken by the queen of Sheba to gain the wisdom of Solomon; Matt. 12:42.
17. He caused the people to put away the heathen wives whom they had married; Ezra 9:1—10:14.
18. "Than great riches"; Prov. 22:1.
19. The petition of James and John to sit beside Christ in his glory; Mark 10:35-45.
20. In order to defeat Baasha of the Northern Kingdom he formed an alliance with a heathen, Ben-hadad, King of Syria; 2 Chron. 16:1-6.
21. Job (19:25).
22. Opening the eyes of blind Bartimæus; Mark 10:46-52.
23. When Christ sent for the colt on which to ride into Jerusalem; Mark 11:1-6.
24. The cursing of the barren fig-tree; Mark 11:12-14, 20-22.
25. When a Pharisee criticised him for omitting the ceremonial washings before dinner; Luke 11:37-40.
26. The parable of the friend at midnight; Luke 11:5-13.
27. Mary of Bethany; John 12:1-8.
28. His hand dried up; 1 Kings 13:1-10.
29. "Train up a child in the way he should go"; Prov. 22:6.
30. Christ's triumphal entry into Jerusalem; Mark 11:9, 10.
31. The prophet who rebuked King Asa for allying himself with Ben-hadad, king of Syria; 2 Chron. 16:7-10.
32. With Malachi's clear prophecy of John the Baptist; Mal. 4:5, 6; compare Matt. 11:14.
33. The Pharisees who believed on Christ but did not dare to confess him; John 12:42, 43.
34. Elah; 1 Kings 16:9, 10.
35. Just before the Lord's Supper, in order to rebuke them for their strife for precedence; John 13:1-15.
36. King Omri; 1 Kings 16:23, 24.
37. Zimri; 1 Kings 16:15.
38. In his discourse at the Last Supper; John 14:6.
39. Fourteen years; Gen. 29:18-30.
40. In his discourse at the Last Supper; John 14:26.
41. The benediction is Gen. 31:49, and it was originally a witness between Laban and Jacob.
42. At Antioch in Pisidia; Acts 13:14-42.
43. The image was made by Aaron and destroyed by Moses; Ex. 32:1-20.
44. At Antioch in Pisidia; Acts 13:44-48.
45. Her sister Leah; Gen. 29:25-28.
46. When his face shone after talking with God on Mt. Sinai; Ex. 34:29-35.
47. In 1 Cor. 12, the entire chapter.
48. At Mahanaim; Gen. 32:1, 2.
49. 1 Cor. 13.
50. 1 Cor. 15.

SERIES XXVIII.

1. Solomon's Song 8:7.
2. He was talking about the possibility of a rich man—*e. g.*, the rich young ruler—entering the kingdom of God; Mark 10:26, 27.
3. The raising of Lazarus from the dead; John 11.
4. When the Seventy were out working for him; Luke 10:17, 18.
5. In Malachi (3:8-10).
6. From Bethphage, on the Mount of Olives; Mark 11:1.
7. He wrestled all night with an angel, until the angel by a touch put his thigh out of joint; Gen. 32:22-32.
8. Rebekah's nurse; Gen. 35:8.
9. Samson, the Judge; Judg. 14:5, 6, etc.
10. Joseph; Gen. 37:3.
11. By letting him down through a window and putting an image in the bed in his place; 1 Sam. 19:12-17.
12. Joseph, Gen. 30:22-24; Benjamin, Gen. 35; 16-19.
13. Ahab and his wife Jezebel, an idolatress, daughter of the king of the Sidonians; 1 Kings 16:28-33.
14. In Gilead; 1 Kings 17:1.
15. The feeding of the five thousand.
16. Joseph; Gen. 37:5, etc.
17. To Peter, after his failure to walk on the water; Matt 14:30, 31.
18. Samson; Judg. 14:5-18.
19. The Pharisees; Matt. 15:14.
20. Peter, at Christ's bidding; Matt. 17:24-27.
21. Jonathan; 1 Sam. 20:18-42.
22. Zarephath; 1 Kings 17:8-10.
23. At Dothan; Gen. 37:17.
24. Peter; Matt. 16:19.
25. Hidden in the temple; 2 Kings 11:1-3.
26. When Jacob wished to make an impression on his wronged brother Esau; Gen. 32:13-21.
27. Four hundred and ninety times—seventy times seven; that is, indefinitely; Matt. 18:21, 22.
28. Christ's parable of the laborer who was not hired till the eleventh hour, yet received a day's pay; Matt. 20:1-16.
29. The parable of the ten virgins; Matt. 25:1-13.
30. It was a cave where David's outlaws lived with him; 1 Sam. 22:1, 2.
31. Of his day of judgment; Matt. 25:31-46.
32. Reuben, Gen. 37:21, 22; and Judah, Gen. 37:26, 27.
33. Multiplied her meal and oil and restored her son to life; 1 Kings 17:10-24.
34. Samson; Judg. 15:15-17.
35. Caiaphas; Matt. 26:3.
36. The Pharaoh who slew King Josiah at Megiddo; 2 Kings 23:29.
37. By cutting off Saul's robe in the cave of En-gedi, 1 Sam. 24:1-22; and by taking the spear and cruse from beside Saul as he slept, 1 Sam. 26:5-25.
38. For thirty pieces of silver (about $19.50); Matt. 26:15.
39. Athaliah; 2 Kings 11:1.
40. The Last Supper; Matt. 26:30.
41. A hypocritical pretence of friendship or love, as Judas betrayed Christ with a kiss; Luke 23:47, 48.
42. Lystra.
43. The angel gave it, after Jacob wrestled with him; Gen. 32:28.
44. The servant of the high priest whose ear Peter cut off; but Christ healed it; John 18:10, 11; Luke 22:51.
45. Potiphar; Gen. 39:1-6.
46. James the brother of our Lord; Acts 15:13-21.
47. High priest under Athaliah and Joash; he was leader in placing Joash on the throne; 2 Kings 11:4-21.
48. Silas took the place of Barnabas, Acts 15:40; Timothy took the place of Mark, Acts 16:1-3.
49. Peter denied Christ three times and the cock crew twice; Mark 14:29-31, 66-72.
50. The wife of churlish Nabal, who made amends by being kind to David, and who later married him; 1 Sam. 25:1-42.

SERIES XXIX.

1. "I am the resurrection and the life," etc.; John 11:25, 26.
2. The kindly Ethiopian who pulled Jeremiah by cords out of the dungeon; Jer. 38:7-13.
3. It commemorates Christ's triumphal entry into Jerusalem, when the multitude strewed palm branches in his way; John 12:13.
4. Aunt of Joash, who preserved the young prince by hiding him for seven years in the temple; 2 Kings 11:1-3.
5. The chief butler was restored, the chief baker executed; Gen. 40:20-22.
6. Delilah; Judg. 16:1-21.
7. "Render to Cæsar the things that are Cæsar's, and to God the things that are God's"; Mark 12:17.
8. The Philistines; 1 Sam. 27:1-12.
9. The wife of Joseph; Gen. 41:45.
10. She put into the temple treasury *two* mites, which was all her possessions; Mark 12:41-44.
11. David's generous treatment of the portion of his men who were not able to join in pursuing the enemy; 1 Sam. 30:9-25.
12. When his feet were anointed with precious ointment at the house of Simon the leper; Mark 14:3-9.
13. The witch of En-dor; 1 Sam. 28:7-25.
14. Manasseh and Ephraim; Gen. 41:50-52.
15. Gethsemane, meaning "oil-press"; Mark 14:32.
16. Because the Sanhedrin had no power to order an execution; only the Roman governor could do that; Mark 15:1.
17. (1) "Father, forgive them, for they know not what they do"; Luke 23:34. (2) "Verily I say unto thee, To-day shalt thou be with me in paradise"; Luke 23:43. (3) "Woman, behold thy Son! . . . . Behold thy mother"; John 19:26, 27. (4) "My God, my God, why hast thou forsaken me?"; Matt. 27:46. (5) "I thirst"; John 19:28. (6) "It is finished"; John 19:30. (7) "Father, into thy hands I commend my spirit"; Luke 23:46.
18. Barabbas, an insurrectionist and murderer; Mark 15:6-11.
19. Gaza; Judg. 16:21-31.
20. Judah; Gen. 44:33.
21. Simon of Cyrene in North Africa; Mark 15:21.
22. For searching the Scriptures; Acts 17:10, 11.
23. The son and successor of Saul; 2 Sam. 2:8-10.
24. Golgotha (Hebrew) and Calvary (Latin), both meaning "the place of a skull," derived from its skull-like appearance; Mark 15:22.
25. The inscription on an altar: "To the Unknown God"; Acts 17:23.
26. David, in his lament for Jonathan; 2 Sam. 1:26.
27. In the land of Goshen; Gen. 47:1-6.
28. Said by Christ to his disciples just before his ascension; Mark 16:15.
29. David, in lamenting the death of Saul's general, Abner; 2 Sam. 3:38.
30. In Jacob's dying words; Gen. 49:10.
31. In Troas (Troy); Acts 16:8-10.
32. "In the name of the Father, and of the Son, and of the Holy Ghost": Matt. 28:19.
33. Because Paul had cured a demoniac slave girl used for divination; Acts 17:16-24.
34. Thessalonica; Acts 17:1-9.
35. Said of Joseph in Jacob's dying words; Gen. 49:24.
36. On Mars' Hill (the Areopagus); Acts 17:19.
37. Because he laid hands on the ark to steady it as it was being transported to Jerusalem; 2 Sam. 6:1-11.
38. With Aquila and his wife Priscilla, because they were tentmakers like him; Acts 18:1-3.
39. Gallio; Acts 18:12-16.
40. An eloquent and able Christian, but poorly instructed; Acts 18:24-28.
41. Joseph of Arimathæa, a member of the Sanhedrin; Luke 23:50-53.

SERIES XXIX.—Continued.

42. In the school of Tyrannus; Acts 19: 8-10.
43. Eutychus at Troy (Troas), who in his sleep fell from a third story window; Acts 20; 6-12.
44. In Proverbs (23:29-35).
45. At Miletus; Acts 20:17-38.
46. Obadiah; 1 Kings 18:3, 13.
47. The riot of the silversmiths whose trade in heathen shrines Paul was injuring; Acts 19:23-34.
48. On Mt. Carmel; 1 Kings 18:19.
49. By making a great bonfire of their costly books of magic, worth 50,000 pieces of silver; Acts 19:18-20.
50. He wished to erect a splendid temple in Jerusalem, but the prophet Nathan forbade him; 2 Sam. 7:1-29.

SERIES XXX.

1. "Then am I strong"; 2 Cor. 12:10.
2. Malachi (4:2).
3. Eve; Abel; Jonathan; Martha; James; Barnabas (or Silas, or Timothy); Sapphira; Naomi; Elisha; Priscilla.
4. The son of Jonathan, lame in both feet, whom David cherished for his father's sake.
5. "It is more blessed to give than to receive," from Paul's farewell address to the Ephesian elders; Acts 20:35.
6. Elijah's challenge to the people on Mt. Carmel; 1 Kings 18:21.
7. Philip the evangelist; Acts 21:8, 9.
8. One of David's soldiers whose wife, Bathsheba, David took from him, having him abandoned in battle and so slain; 2 Sam. 11:1-27.
9. Tertullus; Acts 24:1-9.
10. The Ephesian seen with Paul in Jerusalem, and the rumor that Paul had brought him into the temple led to the riot and Paul's arrest; Acts 21:29.
11. Christ's parable of the rich fool; Luke 12:16-21.
12. Ananias; Acts 23:1-5.
13. The name, which means "beloved of Jehovah," was bestowed upon Solomon, at God's direction, by Nathan the prophet; 2 Sam. 12:24, 25.
14. Claudius Lysias; Acts 23:26.
15. The coming of the storm, after Elijah's contest on Mt. Carmel; 1 Kings 18:44.
16. The first was Felix, Acts 24:3; and the second was Festus, Acts 25:1.
17. At Joab's command, she brought about a reconciliation between David and Absalom; 2 Sam. 14:1-33.
18. Felix; Acts 24:25.
19. Elijah's despondency in the wilderness, in his flight from Jezebel; 1 Kings 19:4.
20. Herod (Antipas); Luke 13:31, 32.
21. Absalom; 2 Sam. 15:1-14.
22. King Agrippa; Acts 26:19.
23. Christ's parable of the great supper; Luke 14:15-24.
24. The prodigal son; Luke 15:11-32.
25. The Old Testament Judas, David's wise counsellor, who joined in Absalom's rebellion, and, when his counsel was rejected, committed suicide; 2 Sam. 16:15—17:23.
26. Paul's beautiful letter to Philemon asks him to receive back his runaway slave, Onesimus.
27. The parable of the rich man and Lazarus; Luke 16:19-31.
28. One of Saul's family, who cursed and stoned David on his withdrawal from Jerusalem in Absalom's rebellion; 2 Sam. 16:5-13.
29. The parable of the Pharisee and publican; Luke 18:9-14.
30. Zacchæus, a publican of Jericho; Luke 19:1-9.
31. As he rode in the battle through a thick wood his head was caught in the branch of an oak; there Joab found him and killed him; 2 Sam. 18:8-17.

SERIES XXX.—Continued.

32. The wife of King Agrippa; Acts 25:13.
33. Pilate and Herod; Luke 23:12.
34. Greek, Latin, and Hebrew; Luke 23:38.
35. Mourning; David went there to mourn for Absalom; 2 Sam. 18:33.
36. Elijah's experience on Mt. Horeb; 1 Kings 19:12.
37. The centurion in whose charge Paul sailed to Rome; Acts 27:1.
38. To Emmaus; one of them was Clopas; Luke 24:13-35.
39. The drink of the Bethlehem well, which three of his warriors risked their lives to bring him; 2 Sam. 23:14-17.
40. "Are the feet of him that bringeth good tidings, that publisheth peace"; Isa. 52:7.
41. Of Elijah's appointment of Elisha as his successor; 1 Kings 19:19.
42. Jehoshaphat; 1 Kings 22:29-37.
43. The owner of vineyard which Ahab wished, and because Naboth would not sell it the king had him slain; 1 Kings 21:1-29.
44. Ezra 7:21.
45. Said by Paul in giving an account of his vision on the way to Rome; Acts 27:23.
46. Esth. 8:9.
47. On the island of Melita (Malta); Acts 28:1.
48. Sixty-six Books, 1,189 chapters, 31,173 verses, 773,692 words, and 3,586,489 letters.
49. The chief man of Malta, whose father Paul healed; Acts 28:7-10.
50. Ps. 118:8.

TOPICAL QUIZZES

(Roman numerals refer to Series; Arabic numerals to questions in the Series.)

I. A GEOGRAPHICAL QUIZ.

I: 1; 8; 16; 25; 35; 44.—II: 19; 36; 38; 42; 46.—III: 14; 21; 27.—IV: 1; 9; 18; 23; 25; 27; 28; 34; 39; 50.—V: 12; 14; 30.—VI: 1; 5; 11; 21; 30; 45; 49.—VII: 17; 24; 29; 46; 48.—VIII: 7; 10; 48.—IX: 1; 12; 49.—X: 1; 24; 46.—XI: 7; 13; 17; 20; 22; 36; 43.—XII: 2; 5; 9; 19; 29; 33.—XIII: 5; 8; 22; 29; 45.—XIV: 1; 32; 44.—XV: 1; 18; 19; 33.—XVI: 11; 14; 15.—XVII: 28; 42; 50.—XVIII: 2; 16; 19; 24; 29; 44; 46; 47.—XIX: 28; 29; 37; 49.—XX: 10; 19; 23; 26; 28; 40; 47.—XXI: 8.—XXII: 10; 30; 32; 42; 44.—XXIII: 4; 10; 22; 27; 41.—XXIV: 6; 11.—XXV: 20; 25; 27; 30.—XXVI: 31; 32; 37; 46..—XXVII: 36; 42; 44; 48.—XXVIII: 6; 14; 22; 23; 30; 42.—XXIX: 15; 19; 24; 27; 31; 36; 45; 48.

II. A QUIZ ON MEN OF THE OLD TESTAMENT.

I: 10; 11; 29; 38.—II: 1; 2; 4; 8; 14; 24; 26; 37.—III: 2; 13; 34; 37; 40; 46.—IV: 2; 3; 16; 24.—V: 9; 10; 20; 42.—VI: 1; 19; 22; 38; 50.—VII: 6, 8; 11; 30; 33; 37.—VIII: 12; 14; 28; 31; 35; 37.—IX: 2; 6; 9; 20; 25; 27; 44.—X: 6; 8; 17; 23; 25; 27; 47.—XI: 3; 12.—XII: 1; 21; 40.—XIII: 7; 10; 16; 31; 32; 44; 50.—XIV: 22: 24; 39.— XV: 2; 12; 14; 21; 25; 36.—XVI: 5; 12; 17; 21; 25; 29.—XVII: 5; 37.—XVIII: 20; 22; 39; 48.—XIX: 18; 25; 34; 42; 44.—XX: 1; 42; 49.—XXI: 2; 4; 6.—XXII: 31; 39; 40; 48.—XXIII: 7; 13; 16; 23; 33; 35.—XXIV: 4; 24; 25; 34.—XXV: 4; 16; 19; 32; 35; 36; 41; 43.—XXVI: 39; 41; 47; 49.—XXVII: 9; 14; 39.—XXVIII: 9; 10; 12; 16; 18; 21; 32; 34; 45; 47.—XXIX: 2; 5; 14; 20; 23; 37; 46.—XXX: 4; 8; 13; 21: 25; 28; 31; 40; 43.

III. A QUIZ ON WOMEN OF THE OLD TESTAMENT.

I: 14; 49.—II: 33; 44.—III: 6; 38; 44; 47.—IV: 7; 46.—V: 18; 24.—VI: 17; 23.—VII: 5; 42.—VIII: 1; 5; 15; 23.—IX: 13.—XI: 1; 16; 28; 32.—XII: 48.—XVI: 2; 23.—XVII: 12.—XVIII: 11; 44; 50.—XX: 3.—XXII: 19; 42.—XXIII: 43; 47.—XXIV: 34.—XXV: 47.—XXVI: 44; 47.—XXVII: 45.—XXVIII: 8; 11; 13; 39; 50.—XXIX: 4; 6; 9; 13.—XXX: 17.

IV. A QUIZ ON THE KINGS.

I: 48.—II: 4; 10; 17; 48.—III: 7; 12; 16; 43.—IV: 12; 21.—V: 28.—VI: 8; 35; 47.—VII: 6; 9; 32; 36; 41.—VIII: 24; 46.—IX: 18; 24.—X: 38.—XI: 11; 14; 25; 30.—XIII: 27.—XIV: 8; 26.—XV: 3.—XVI: 32.—XVII: 23; 30; 33.—XIX: 39; 41; 45.—XXI: 1; 10.—XXII: 25; 46.—XXIII: 20; 26; 31.—XXIV: 9; 13; 15.—XXV: 33; 39; 44.—XXVI.—1; 42.—XXVII: 7; 20; 28; 34; 37.—XXVIII: 13; 25; 36.—XXIX: 50.—XXX: 42.

V. A QUIZ ON THE PROPHETS.

I: 2; 12; 18. 46.—II: 2; 42.—III: 10; 15; 19; 25; 29; 31; 45.—IV: 14; 48.—V: 3; 45; 47.—VI: 3; 40; 41; 44; 48; 49.—VII: 2; 39; 50.—VIII: 11; 27; 36; 38.—IX: 5; 13; 22; 49.—X: 34.—XI: 28.—XIII: 25.—XV: 30.—XVI: 28; 36; 41.—XVII: 9.—XVIII: 41; 43; 47; 49.—XX: 18; 21; 24; 27.—XXI: 12; 28.—XXII: 7, 27; 28; 44.—XXIII: 29.—XXVI: 3; 16; 19.—XXVII: 31.—XXVIII: 33.

VI. A QUIZ ON MEN OF THE NEW TESTAMENT.

1: 42.—II: 13; 16.—III: 4; 10; 36.—IV: 11; 30; 40; 42; 47.—V: 19.—VI: 19; 29.—IX: 7; 43; 45; 48.—X: 2; 28; 48.—XI: 24; 31; 34; 46; 49.—XII: 14.—XIII: 23.—XIV: 4; 19.—XV: 45.—XVI: 16; 30; 43; 44; 47.—XVII: 32; 36; 49.—XVIII: 21.—XIX: 23; 40.—XX: 14; 16; 17; 22; 25.—XXI: 21; 44; 48.—XXII: 9; 35.—XXIV: 48.—XXV: 3; 6; 8; 38.—XXVI: 10; 23; 26; 30; 38.—XXVII: 2; 3.—XXVIII: 35; 44; 46; 48.—XXIX: 18; 21; 38; 39; 40; 41; 43.—XXX: 7; 9; 10; 12; 14; 16; 18; 20; 22; 26; 30; 33; 37; 38; 49.

VII. A QUIZ ON WOMEN OF THE NEW TESTAMENT.

I: 27.—III: 42; 44.—VI: 33.—IX: 42.—X: 20.—XII: 13.—XIV: 16; 30.—XVII: 46.—XIX: 12; 43.—XX: 31; 48; 50.—XXI: 3; 34; 39.—XXV: 18; 23.—XXVI: 31.—XXVII: 27.—XXIX: 38.—XXX: 7; 32.

VIII. A QUIZ ON CHRIST'S DISCIPLES.

I: 9; 26; 37.—II: 20.—V: 25; 31; 43.—VI: 20; 24; 27; 43.—VII: 10; 13.—XI: 21; 23; 33; 50.—XII: 22.—XIII: 21.—XIV: 10; 23.—XV: 24; 28; 35.—XVII: 38.—XVIII: 17; 25.—XIX: 46; XX: 16; 26.—XXI: 7.—XXII: 20.—XXIII: 28; 30; 36; 42; 46.—XXV: 34.—XXVI: 21.—XXVIII: 17; 20; 24; 38; 49.

IX. A QUIZ ON OBJECTS, ANIMALS, PLANTS, ETC.

I: 4; 12; 13; 19; 25; 31; 43; 50.—II: 16; 41.—IV: 6; 37.—V: 15; 48.—VI: 14; 31.—VII: 12.—VIII: 4; 5; 6; 18; 25; 39.—IX: 17; 19; 33; 40; 46.—X: 14; 19; 26.—XII: 23.—XIII: 14.—XIV: 9; 29.—XV: 47.—XVII: 21.—XVIII: 23.—XIX: 31; 50; XXII: 5; 14; 33.—XXIV: 39.—XXX: 19

X. A TABERNACLE AND TEMPLE QUIZ.

I: 15.—II: 28; 37; 49.—IV: 19; 44.—V: 8; 13; 37.—VI: 26; 38.—VII: 28; 38.—VIII: 8; 41; 44; 45.—IX: 47.—X: 7; 22; 31.—XI: 15; 19; 38.—XIII: 34; 40; 42.—XIV: 2; 11; 21; 31; 48.—XV: 4; 27.—XVI: 9; 20.—XVII: 3: 39; 48.—XVIII: 3; 10.—XIX: 9; 11.—XXI: 16.—XXIV: 18.—XXV: 26; 29.—XXVI: 17: 34.

XI. A SLICED-QUOTATIONS QUIZ.—OLD TESTAMENT.

I: 5; 17; 40.—II: 3.—III: 8; 28; 35.—IV: 4; 41.—V: 1; 23; 44.—VI: 10; 32; 39.—VII: 44; 47; 49.—VIII: 3; 20, 22; 32; 34; 49; 50.—IX: 4; 14; 23; 29.—X: 10; 39; 42; 49.—XI: 35; 48.—XII: 10.—XIII: 2; 4; 33; 39.—XIV: 27.—XV: 6; 41; 44; 49.—XVI: 31; 39.—XVII: 4; 11; 17; 25; 34; 40.—XVIII: 26; 28; 36.—XX: 6; 11; 13; 30.—XXII: 13; 41.—XXIII: 39.—XXIV: 23; 26; 33; 45; 46.—XXVI: 7.—XXVII: 4; 12; 15; 18; 29.

XII. A SLICED-QUOTATIONS QUIZ. NEW TESTAMENT.

I: 34; 41; 45.—II: 25; 40.——IV: 20.—V: 29; 34; 40; 46; 49.—VII: 16; 22; 40; 43.—VIII: 30.—IX: 10; 15; 21; 26; 38.—X: 13; 16; 18; 40; 50.—XI: 5; 45; 47.—XII: 27.—XIII: 9; 30; 37.—XIV: 17; 34; 35; 47.—XV: 5; 15; 17.—XVI: 42; 48.—XVII: 1; 18.—XVIII: 4; 13; 31.—XIX: 13.—XX: 9; 33.—XXI: 11; 17; 19; 20; 26; 33; 35.—XXII: 12; 23.—XXIII: 2; 12; 18; 21; 34; 38; 49.—XXIV: 2; 10; 41.—XXV: 14; 50.—XXX: 1.

XIII. A QUIZ ON BIBLE BOOKS.

I: 3; 6.—II: 5; 9; 11; 15; 23; 31; 39; 43;. 50.—III: 1; 4; 5; 9; 19; 20.—IV: 5; 8; 22; 31; 43.—V: 6; 11.—VI: 6.—VII; 1; 7; 20.—IX: 11.—XIV: 40.—XVII: 7.—XX: 34.—XXI: 32; 37.—XXII: 11.—XXIII: 17; 24.—XXIV: 1; 14; 17; 20; 49.—XXV: 12; 46.—XXVI: 36.—XXVII: 11.—XXX: 26; 48.

XIV. A QUIZ ON SPLENDID PASSAGES.

I: 22; 23; 28; 32; 33; 39.—II: 6.—IV: 13; 15; 32; 37.—V: 39.—VI: 9; 37; 46.—IX: 11.—X: 26; 37.—XI: 9; 26; 44.—XII: 11; 12; 32.—XIII: 19; 43.—XIV: 45.—XV: 13; 29.—XVI: 3.—XVII: 2.—XVIII: 7; 18.—XIX: 17; 20.—XX: 2; 36.—XXI: 9; 13; 14; 38; 40.—XXIV: 27; 31.—XXVI: 15; 22; 28; 33.—XXVII: 6; 8; 32; 47; 49; 50.—XXVIII: 5.—XXIX: 44.—XXX: 24.

XV. A QUIZ ON FAMOUS SAYINGS.

I: 2; 7.—II: 7; 27; 32; 35; 45.—III: 3; 13; 24; 26; 48.—V: 7; 38.—VI: 4; 7; 13; 23; 29; 40; 43.—VII: 8; 11; 14; 35; 42.—VIII: 12; 15; 26; 42.—IX: 8; 34; 39; 41; 50.—X: 3; 4; 12; 21; 29; 30;

33.—XI: 2; 6; 37; 40; 41.—XII: 6; 7; 8; 15; 16; 17; 28; 35; 39; 44; 46; 49.—XIII: 3; 6; 15; 17; 18; 24; 26; 28; 36; 49.—XIV: 5; 12; 13; 16; 18; 28; 38; 43.—XV: 8; 9; 16; 26; 32; 34; 39; 43.—XVI: 8; 22; 24; 38.—XVII: 10; 14; 35; 41; 43; 46.—XVIII: 1; 9; 15; 34; 35.—XIX: 3; 10; 15; 30; 33; 36; 47.—XX: 32; 41; 43; 45; 46.—XXI: 18; 24; 31; 45.—XXII: 1; 3; 4; 17; 18; 30; 36; 37; 38; 45; 47.—XXIII: 1; 3; 5; 19; 25; 37.—XXIV: 7; 12; 21; 22; 35; 37; 40.—XXV: 7; 13; 17; 22; 24; 31; 40; 45; 48.—XXVI: 2; 6; 8; 12; 18; 25.—XXVII: 1; 23; 33; 38.—XXVIII: 2; 29.—XXIX: 1; 12; 26; 29; 34; 35.—XXX: 5; 6; 11; 29.

XVI. A QUIZ ON NOTABLE VERSES.

I: 21; 24.—III: 30; 32; 33; 49.—IV: 10; 29; 35.—V: 26.—VI: 12; 18; 25; 28; 36.—VII: 3; 18.—VIII: 13; 16; 19; 33.—IX: 9; 16; 31; 32; 35.—X: 5; 44; 45.—XI: 18; 39.—XII: 18; 31; 47.—XIII: 11; 13; 41.—XIV: 20; 33; 37; 49.—XV: 11.—XVI: 18; 33; 35; 46; 49; 50.—XVII: 6; 13; 15; 22; 31; 45.—XVIII: 38; 42; 45; 49.—XIX: 5; 7; 32.—XX: 12; 15; 29; 35; 37; 44.—XXI: 5; 30; 36; 42; 47; 49.—XXII: 6; 8; 16; 22; 24; 26; 50.—XXIII: 8; 11; 14; 15; 32; 44; 45; 48.—XXIV: 16; 28; 29; 36; 43; 44; 50.—XXV: 1; 2; 5; 9; 10; 11; 21; 28; 49.—XXVI: 4; 5; 9; 14; 48.—XXVII: 21; 26; 30; 41.—XXVIII: 1.—XXIX: 7; 28; 32.—XXX: 2; 22; 40; 44; 46; 50.

XVII. A QUIZ ON FAMOUS PHRASES.

I: 20; 47.—II: 34.—III: 39.—IV: 11; 17; 33; 38; 49.—V: 19; 32; 36; 50.—VI: 34; 42.—VII: 19; 50.—VIII: 9; 17; 29.—IX: 30; 37.—XII: 26; 43.—XIII: 20; 47.—XIV: 7; 36; 42; 50.—XV: 7; 22; 38.—XVI: 6; 7; 13; 27; 40.—XVII: 19; 27.—XVIII: 8; 14; 27; 32; 37.—XIX: 1; 2; 4; 6; 14; 27; 38; 48.—XX: 8; 20; 38; 39.—XXI: 22; 50.—XXII: 14; 49.—XXIII: 6; 9; 40; 50.—XXIV: 30.—XXV: 15; 37.—XXVI: 11; 20; 27; 29; 35; 40; 43; 45.—XXVII: 5; 10; 19; 25.—XXVIII: 19; 28; 31; 41.—XXIX: 10; 11; 30.—XXX: 15; 23; 27; 45.

XVIII. A QUIZ ON THE MEANINGS OF NAMES.

II: 9; 22; 26; 29; 44.—III: 17.—IV: 1; 5; 22; 27.—V: 5; 27.—VII: 1; 15.—X: 15.—XII: 3.—XIII: 35.—XVI: 4.—XIX: 4.—XXI: 41.—XXIV: 24; 25.—XXVI: 37.—XXIX: 15; 24.

XIX. A COMPREHENSIVE QUIZ.

II: 12; 18; 21.—III: 5.—V: 2.—VII: 2.—XI: 33.—XII: 42; 50.—XV: 48.—XVII: 28.—XXIX: 17.—XXX: 3.

XX. A QUIZ ON EVENTS.

I: 11; 18; 30; 36.—II: 28; 47; 48.—III: 31; 45; 50.—IV: 12; 26; 44.—V: 4; 17; 33.—VII: 17; 21; 26; 31; 34; 45.—VIII: 2; 21; 40; 43.—IX: 12.—X: 11; 32; 35; 36; 41; 43.—XI: 8; 27; 29; 38; 42.—XII: 4; 25; 34; 36; 38; 45.—XIII: 1; 38; 48.—XIV: 3; 15; 25.—XV: 20; 31; 37; 42; 46.—XVI: 19; 26; 45.—XVIII: 6; 12; 19; 23; 30.—XIX: 8; 16; 19; 21; 44.—XX: 4; 5; 7.—XXI: 15; 23; 27; 29.—XXII: 2; 21.—XXIV: 8; 18; 38; 42; 47.—XXVI: 24; 50.—XXVII: 13; 16; 17; 22; 24; 35; 40; 43; 46.—XXVIII: 3; 4; 7; 26; 37; 40; 43.—XXIX: 3; 8; 16; 25; 33; 42; 47; 49.—XXX: 36; 39; 41.

XXI. A MISCELLANEOUS QUIZ.

II: 30.—III: 11; 18; 20; 22; 23; 41.—IV: 36; 45.—V: 16; 21; 22; 35; 41; 47.—VI: 15; 16.—VII: 4; 23; 25; 27.—VIII: 47.—IX: 3; 28; 36.—X: 9.—XI: 4; 10.—XII: 20; 24; 30; 37; 41.—XIII: 12; 46.—XIV: 6; 14; 41; 46.—XV: 10; 23; 40; 50.—XVI: 1; 10; 34; 37.—XVII: 8; 16; 20; 24; 26; 28; 44; 47.—XVIII: 5; 33; 40.—XIX: 22; 24; 26; 35.—XXI: 25; 43; 46.—XXII: 15; 29; 32; 34; 43.—XXIV: 3; 5; 19; 32.—XXV: 42.—XXVI: 13.—XXVIII: 15; 27.—XXIX: 22.—XXX: 34; 35.